Teaching Sport and Leisure 14+

University Centre at
Blackburn
College

Telephone: 01254 292165

Please return this book on or before the last date shown

Teaching 14+

Series editor: Andy Armitage

Published and forthcoming titles:

Teaching Sport and Leisure 14+

Cliff Huggett and Chris Manley

 Open University Press

Open University Press
McGraw-Hill Education
McGraw-Hill House
Shoppenhangers Road
Maidenhead
Berkshire
England
SL6 2QL

email: enquiries@openup.co.uk
world wide web: www.openup.co.uk

and Two Penn Plaza, New York, NY 10121-2289, USA

First published 2010

A catalogue record of this book is available from the British Library

ISBN-13: 978-0-33-523823-1 (pb) 978-0-33-523824-8 (hb)
ISBN-10: 0335238238 (pb) 0335238246 (hb)

Library of Congress Cataloging-in-Publication Data
CIP data applied for

Typeset by RefineCatch Limited, Bungay, Suffolk
Printed in the UK by CPI Antony Rowe, Chippenham, Wiltshire

The **McGraw·Hill** Companies

Contents

List of figures

List of tables

List of boxes

Series editor's preface

For historical reasons perhaps, subject pedagogy for Post 16 teachers has not been considered a professional development priority. The possession of appropriate academic or vocational qualifications and experience have traditionally been considered sufficient for those teaching older students assumed themselves to possess the motivation and skills for effective learning. However, the increasing numbers of 14–16 year olds taking part of their programmes in FE colleges, the rise in the participation rate of 16–19 year olds and the increasing number of 18–30 year olds having experience of higher education, have created a large and diverse population in all sector institutions presenting a challenge to those teaching Post 14 students. Both the 2003 and 2006 Ofsted surveys of Post 16 teacher training and the 2007 reforms of initial teacher training and continuing professional development, have drawn attention to the urgent need for both new and existing teachers to receive training to teach their subject or curriculum specialism and to receive support from subject coaches or mentors in the workplace. Most of the programmes preparing the 40,000 trainees annually to teach in the lifelong learning sector are generic in nature, rather than subject specific.

Partly because of the Institute for Learning's requirements regarding both CPD and professional formation, there is considerable growth in in-service continuing professional development and, given the attention given by both Ofsted and DCSF to subject pedagogy as described above, it is likely that there will be a sharp CPD focus for many colleges on subject teaching, particularly since much of the burden of subject based training will fall on the shoulders of FE college based mentors. The increase in vocational education in schools, particularly with the introduction of diplomas, will see a growing need for secondary PGCE students and existing 14–18 secondary teachers to enhance their subject pedagogy for 14+ students. One of the key recommendations of a recent report on vocational teacher training[1] is that "Vocational and applied pedagogies should become a research priority and be embedded within school, further education (FE) and higher education (HE) initial teacher training (ITT) and continuing professional development (CPD)."

---

[1] The Skills Commission (2010) *An Inquiry into Teacher training in Vocational Education* London: The Skills Commission P.14

Each series title is therefore aimed to act as support for teachers, whether on a formal initial or CPD programme or simply as a guide for those teaching the subject on a daily basis in one of a variety of possible contexts: secondary, FE, Adult and Community Education, work-based training. Chapters in each title follow a similar format. Chapter 1 deals with the nature of subject(s) in the curriculum area, considering any contesting conceptions of what the subject should be about, as well as current issues connected with teaching it. There is a focus on subject updating, identifying recent key developments in subjects as well as the means for students to be able to update themselves. Chapter 2 provides an introduction to the major programmes in the subject area focussing mainly on those in the National Qualifications Framework such as GCSE, AS, Key Skills, NVQ, Diplomas, although reference is made to the Framework for Higher Education Qualifications. There is a consideration of the central features of each programme such as aims and objectives, unitisation or modularity, content. The chapter also guides readers in the task of turning syllabus into learning via schemes of work. The third chapter considers key skills and functional skills, looking at differing models of skills development and how such skills might be taught through the subject. Chapter 4 looks at the teaching and learning strategies most often used in the curriculum area. There are clearly certain learning and teaching strategies that are used universally across post 14 programmes – lectures, discussion, presentations are the most obvious. Even these, however, will need to be treated in the context of their use in the subject area. Presentations which model those in advertising or marketing might be effective learning strategies in an AS Media Studies or Applied Business GCSE, whereas in Key Skills Communications they might have the purpose of developing oracy skills and as part of an Access course of developing study skills. Chapter 5 considers resources as used in the context of the curriculum area. When audio-visual resources are being considered, for example, students might be presented with exemplar handouts and PowerPoint presentations with subject-related content. ICT resources should be considered in terms of their strengths in relation to the subject. Are there good commercial software packages, for example? How can they best be used for teaching? What are the key web sites relating to the subject area? How might searching best be carried out? There is a consideration of the range of published resources available in the subject area, with examples of how material is presented and how use of it is structured. Chapter 6 offers guidance on the role of the teacher as assessor in the programmes identified in Chapter 2, with a particular emphasis on the range of assessment strategies used as part of these programmes.

Each title features a range of pedagogical features which might be useful alone, in pairs or in groups. Readers are invited for example to reflect, discuss, respond to a range of visual stimuli, give short answer responses to questions, consider case studies, complete short tasks.

One of the most striking features of Cliff Huggett and Chris Manley's *Teaching Sport and Leisure* is their establishment of both sport and leisure as major areas of human activity and as central to our national and global lives. Traditionally, these areas have been marginalised in curricula and their teaching regarded as a matter of training, instruction and drilling but the growth in the curriculum has reflected their increasing importance in society and the authors are able to describe the rich pedagogical opportunities for teachers and their students in these exciting subject areas. Sport and Leisure are shown to have great potential to offer a wide range of learners meaningful, relevant and highly motivating contexts and activities for learning inside and outside the classroom, whether on an educational field trip or visit or in the work place. The authors also clearly show their potential as subject areas to develop a wide range of skills, whether they be the functional skills of English, Maths and ICT or the softer, wider key skills or Personal Learning and Thinking Skills.

Andy Armitage

Preface

Returning to the office after a long day of teaching Leisure and Tourism to students on our 14–19 PGCE programme, I was bemoaning the fact that there were no textbooks that addressed the specific pedagogical issues relating to the subject to back up my own teaching. 'Then write one!' said the Head of Department, Andy Armitage, who is now series editor for this set of texts on the pedagogy of vocational subjects. Two years later, after steadily trying to avoid the commitment, this idea has become a reality.

From the earliest days of my teaching career as a PE teacher, I found myself questioning accepted pedagogies of my subject. Why was traditional gymnastics the central pillar of the PE programme in those days? What would be a more meaningful curriculum? Having taught for eleven years in boys' grammar schools, I was then fortunate enough to be placed in a further education environment in which I had virtually carte blanche to develop a curriculum. At the same time, the Sport Leisure and Tourism curriculum was beginning to grow at a national level and I was able to be involved in the development of a variety of curriculum developments such as GNVQs, BTEC Nationals and A levels. Thus my interest in pedagogy and in particular curriculum development began to grow.

With yet another stroke of good fortune, late in my career, I was invited to teach at Canterbury first on PGCE programmes and later on a wide range. So I found a voice, at last, for my passion for the study of pedagogy unconstrained by subject boundaries. In truth, this interests me more than my subject specialism, but teaching on our 14–19 PGCE programme brought together those two areas of my experience: the years as a PE teacher and Sports lecturer in FE, and the pedagogical studies and teaching of my latter years.

So this is what this book is about: how do you teach Sport and Leisure? It is not a book on teaching PE – there are plenty of those around. This is about teaching people who, specifically, are hoping to follow a career in some sphere of the Sport and Leisure industry.

We have tried first to give an overview of what the subject is all about. Certainly, as a subject, it has its detractors in educational circles and in Chapter 1 we have tried to address this by pointing out just how important Sport and Leisure has become to our society today. This then leads us to look at the various programmes that are available to those who want to follow a career in the industry, and then to share with you our experiences of teaching the subject.

I am sure that there will be many of our readers who have, themselves, valuable experiences to share in the same way. I hope that this book will still help you in some way, perhaps to structure those experiences, but we would also like to hear from you so that we can all continue to grow and learn more about this subject which we have been lucky enough to be able to turn into a career.

Cliff Huggett

Acknowledgements

The authors would like to thank all those who have helped and advised us in the preparation of this book. This certainly includes our colleagues in the Post-Compulsory Department at Canterbury Christ Church University and the Sports Department at North West Kent College.

I am particularly appreciative of those who advised me on the chapter on key and functional skills, Jo-Ann Delaney, Amanda Cope and Jane Evershed. They made me realize that importance of embedding the development of the skills into our everyday teaching cannot be underestimated and that, as educators it is something for which we all share a responsibility. But the encouragement I have received and the discussions that I have had with others, such as Andy Armitage, Head of Department and editor of the series, and Gina Donovan, have been invaluable, particularly in those moments of despair when we thought that the project was impossible.

Chris, also, is equally appreciative of his colleagues who have willingly lent him both their time and resources, some of which appear in the book as exemplar materials.

Finally, of course, we would both like to thank those close to us, family and friends who have had to endure our frustrations and long periods of neglect of them, and who, nevertheless, have encouraged us and supported us throughout the project.

1

The context of the Sport and Leisure curriculum and related issues

In this chapter we will be looking at:

- Sport and Leisure as a subject of study
- The scope and variety of the sport and leisure industry
- The knowledge, understanding and skills required to work in the various sectors
- The organization of the industry
- How Sport and Leisure education and training programmes prepare people for employment in the industry
- How learning programmes are affected by national and local initiatives
- The profiles of learners on Sport and Leisure programmes
- The future for Sport and Leisure

Introduction

There are few activities which have secured a more central place in the national culture of countries like Britain and the USA than sport. Loved by millions, it peppers our daily discourse with rich anecdote, vivid terminology and striking imagery. Sporting activities feature prominently in the broadcasting programmes of mass media and they constitute a weighty component of the leisure and entertainment industries. They generate jobs for many people, fortunes for the stars and profits for the business interests involved. Sport stimulates young men [and presumably young women?] to dream of escape from boredom and deprivation. It is eulogised by educators, philanthropists and social reformers, appropriated by politicians and promoted by the modern state.

(Hargreaves 1987: 1)

We have selected this opening paragraph to John Hargreaves' study of *Sport, Power and Culture* because it presents a clear, succinct statement which sums up the importance of Sport and Leisure in our society today in a way that we cannot better.

Sporting competition has been a part of human leisure activity possibly since we started to form social groupings and most of us will be familiar with the images of the Ancient Greek Olympic games and the Roman gladiatorial arenas. But evidence of such sporting competition is not confined to the Greeks and Romans: it may be found in most ancient cultures across the globe, from the steppes of Mongolia to the Andes of South America, and in many cases this has been a highly organized activity.

In the nineteenth century in England, sport entered the curriculum of the public schools and, in the twentieth century, grew to become a school subject in its own right as Physical Education. So it continues to grow in importance: pick up any newspaper, turn on the TV and the likelihood is that up to a third (if not more) of their coverage will be sport oriented. There is a government department responsible for sport and leisure activity; vast amounts of money are spent on it; sports performers can earn equally vast sums; businesses invest in sport, sponsoring activities, teams and individuals to advertise their products, and most communities now will provide facilities to make sport and leisure accessible to all.

The importance of Sport and Leisure as a social activity and as an industry, and the organization that is required to sustain it are the subject of this chapter. It is intended to remind readers of the vast scope of the industry; to examine the possibilities for employment and the concomitant skills and knowledge that are necessary to fill those roles as a prelude to considering the impact of all this on teaching and learning in curriculum.

Why 'Sport and Leisure'?

This book is intended to have a broad scope and to address the teaching of the subject and the preparation of those who might wish to work in Sport and Leisure across the whole Lifelong Learning sector. We feel that this title best describes the breadth and perhaps limitations of the subject area that we hope to encompass. It will consider programmes which study not only competitive sport but also those which address the needs of areas such as Community Sports Development, the Health and Fitness Industry and Adventurous Outdoor Activity. The learning line for the 14–19 Diplomas is entitled 'Sport and Active Leisure', but it is important to note that we shall be considering all types of learning programmes in the sector and will not be limiting our discussion to delivery of the Diplomas.

It is, of course, possible that many of our readers will have studied the following topics already at an academic level, but the publication is intended to reach a number of people, some of whom may have little knowledge of the industry. So it is hoped that this brief introduction will convince them of the importance of our subject as an element of the curriculum. For those who are already well informed, it is hoped that this will serve as a reminder of what the subject is all about and act as a stimulus to considering how best to engage their learners in its complexities.

Reflection 1.1

Give five reasons why you think that sport and leisure are important in today's society.

Sport and Leisure as a subject of study

Why are sport and leisure important?

What reasons did you give in reflection 1.1? Perhaps you suggested that they contribute to a healthy lifestyle, or that they provide a controlled outlet for aggression, or encourage good community relations. These may all be true but, in order to get a picture of the breadth of the industry, we shall look at these and many wider issues in the context of sport in society and its role in the economy.

Much of what has been written about Sport and Leisure focuses on the Leisure context. While 'Leisure' does encompass a wide range of both active and passive pursuits, from watching sport to participating in it, or from playing chess to DIY, it is generally acknowledged that Sport and Leisure is a major contributor to this branch of human activity. So it would be useful first to briefly consider the thoughts of important writers on leisure.

Leisure was considered to be an important aspect of life to the Ancient Greeks, for example, Aristotle writing in the fourth century BC claimed that, 'One must have leisure – free from the necessity of being occupied' (Aristotle, in Goodale and Witt 1991: 31). Of course, we should remember that leisure for the Greeks was largely limited to the privileged classes whose experience of leisure was possible through the employment of slave labour. Nevertheless, without this space for leisure, it is possible that we might not have benefitted from the rich cultural heritage of the Ancient Greeks.

Jean Mundy (1998: 57) develops this idea, noting that three founding fathers of Greek philosophy, Socrates, Plato and Aristotle, were each concerned with the need to educate citizens in the 'wise use of leisure'. It was, 'A . . . process through which individuals developed an understanding of the self.' She claims:

> The aim of leisure education is to enable people to reach a relatively high plateau, to have leisure experiences that fall in the upper level of the satisfying, enriching, enhancing end of the life continuum and to be able to attain this level of satisfaction through one's efficacy.
>
> (1998: 21)

So in what ways can leisure activity, and Sport and Leisure in particular, enable us to 'attain this level of satisfaction'?

Sport in society

Sport as a social phenomenon has engaged the interest of many sociologists, politicians and, indeed, as we have seen above, philosophers. Grant Jarvie (2006: 2) observes:

> It is impossible to fully understand contemporary society and culture without acknowledging the place of sport . . . It is part of the social and cultural fabric of different localities, regions and nations, its transformative potential is evident in some of the poorest areas of the world;

There are many fields of study within the academic discipline of sociology, but we shall focus on those which have an immediate impact on the lives of our learners. Lincoln Allison (1998: 54) critically discusses the view that 'sport reflects society'. 'How odd,' he says, 'even inconceivably odd, if it didn't': this is a debate that we can leave the reader to pursue at their leisure. More important for us is to briefly examine the impact that sport has on society generally in both positive and negative ways.

To paraphrase Jarvie (2006: 11):

- How can sport transform or intervene to produce social change?
- What is the role of the student and teacher in enabling this?

The argument that Jarvie develops is that sport has the power to liberate and provide opportunities for the underprivileged to assert themselves. For example, while the situation is still far from satisfactory, it does provide a vehicle for women to champion their cause for equality. Undoubtedly, many formerly oppressed ethnic groups have found sport to be a means of expression for their culture. It has become the means to break down some of our class divisions where everyone is seen to be equal on the playing field.

Reflection 1.2

Figure 1.1 is an iconic photo of Nelson Mandela shaking hands with François Pienaar as he hands over the Rugby World Cup trophy: how significant a role has sport played in the development of a multicultural society in South Africa?

Reflection 1.3

Figure 1.2 is a copy of the front page of a programme for the women's international football match between France and the famous Dick Kerr Ladies team from Preston, played in 1920. A crowd of 25,000 watched this match. Why is it still difficult for women to share equal status with men in the sporting arena?

We would add to Jarvie's list the contribution that sport and leisure have made to the health of the nation across all boundaries of society. Undoubtedly, the growing interest in the performance and progress of professional sports teams and individuals does encourage greater public participation: months before the event, the London Marathon brings runners out in their droves, whether they are competing or not; membership of tennis clubs and use of public courts nearly always increase during Wimbledon fortnight, and the success of the British cycling team at the 2008

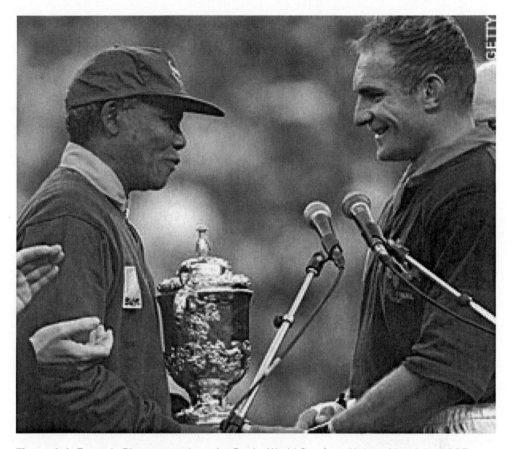

Figure 1.1 François Pienaar receives the Rugby World Cup from Nelson Mandela, 1995
© Getty Images

Olympics encouraged many to return to their bikes. But it has also become fashionable to work out in fitness centres, both private and public for people with no particular objective other than to improve their own levels of health and fitness.

Governments too have been eager to harness the power of sport for good or evil. The Olympic Games of 1936 is probably the most familiar and blatant example of a government using sport as propaganda to pursue its own ends and promote its ideology, but there are many perhaps more subtle examples. On the other hand, sport and leisure has also been seen as important to the cultural identity of nations. Although arising out of colonization of the West Indies by a dominant white 'plantocracy', cricket became a significant part of the indigenous population and 'a symbol of Creole nationalism' (Jarvie 2006: 73).

In the UK, of course, the following for national sports teams is widespread and now includes interest far wider than the traditional football, rugby, cricket and tennis loyalties. Any successes in sports as diverse as rowing, cycling, athletics, swimming, gymnastics, sailing and badminton are applauded with national honours, and bus-top parades are organized arousing national pride. Of course, the cynic will claim that such activities distract the public from the realities of a more mundane and even

Figure 1.2 Programme for the women's football match between Dick Kerr Ladies and the French national team in 1920, which drew a crowd of 25,000 © Dick Kerr Ladies Archives

oppressed existence, but it is to be hoped that they will at least inspire many people to engage in some kind of meaningful physical activity.

Given these possibilities and the growing interest in sport and leisure, it is no wonder that governments and commercial companies are prepared to invest in its development.

Sport and the economy

We would do well here to recall Hargreaves' observation that 'They [sport activities] generate jobs for many people, fortunes for the stars and profits for the business interests involved' (1987: 1). And as Lincoln Allison (1998: 54) observes, 'It is now, broadly defined, the sixth most important industry in Europe.'

Precisely what extent sport and leisure contribute to the economy might be found in the report by the Sport Industry Research Centre (SIRC 2007) at Sheffield Hallam University on the economic importance of sport in England 1985–2005. The report clearly shows the extent of the growth in the industry in that time and gives an indication of the scale of its contribution to the national economy. Currently, sport accounts for 2.6 per cent of total consumer spending, some £14.5bn per annum, or £294 per capita, and employs 1.8 per cent of the total working population, that is equivalent to 434,000 people. Compared with data from 1985, the 'real change' is a staggering growth of 124 per cent and, even taking into account the differences in monetary values, the Gross Added Value (GVA) figures are still impressive. While the data are somewhat skewed by the leap in expenditure on gambling due to tax reform, there has been a marked increase in spending on participation subscriptions and fees and on sport clothing and footwear, both of which would indicate a growth in participation, even taking into account the interest of the fashion industry in sports clothing (Table 1.1).

The importance of this activity to national and local government might also be seen in their figures for income and expenditure. Total income from sport for National Government in 2005 was £6.3bn while expenditure was £1.3bn, and for local government, income was £2.1bn (which included grants from central

Table 1.1 Summary of sport-related consumer spending in England, 1985–2005 (£ m)

	1985	2000	2005
Sport clothing and footwear	595	2,581	3,258
Sports equipment	424	800	1,194
Participation subscriptions and fees	487	2,729	3,469
Admissions to events	71	606	700
Sport-related gambling	891	1,663	3,071
TV rental and satellite subscriptions	51 (in 1990)	1,000	1,579
Other sport-related spending	1,068	2,436	3,311
Total expenditure on sport	3,536	11,815	16,580
Proportion of total consumer expenditure	2.0%	2.3%	2.6%

government and lottery awards) and expenditure was £2.5bn. Clearly, a great deal of importance is attached to sport as an economic, and indeed, a social phenomenon by government, commercial enterprises and individuals.

With our educational programmes in mind, it is perhaps, also, worthwhile break-ing the employment figures down into their various sectors and considering where the dominant occupational roles lie (see Table 1.2). The private commercial sector accounts for 134,000 employees with 32,000 involved in spectator sports and 22,000 in participation sports, the remainder being employed in retailing and the media. The voluntary sector which would include people involved in organizing and coaching in sports clubs, for example, employs 52,000 and the public sector (e.g. local leisure centres and sports development) 51,000.

Table 1.2 Summary of sport-related employment in England, 1985–2005 (000s)

		1985	2000	2005
Commercial sport		97	115	134
	of which			
	Spectator sports	15	35	134
	Participation sports	1	21	22
	Retailing	53	29.7	37
	TV and Radio	3	6	9
Commercial non-sport		144	156	197
Voluntary sector		31	38	52
Public sector		32	37	51
Total sport-related employment		304	365	434
Sport employment as % of total employment		1.3	1.6	1.8

Reflection 1.4

Discussion – what can we learn about public interest in sport and leisure from the data in Tables 1.1 and 1.2? Is the growth in sales of sports clothing in the fashion industry of any significance to our discussion on the importance of sport and leisure?

Clearly, this all indicates a continuing growth in public interest in sport and leisure with a commensurate growth in employment prospects for our learners.

The scope and variety of the Sport and Leisure industry

Many young people choosing to study Sport and Leisure as their main subject in full-time education do so because of the enjoyment and satisfaction that they gain from participation in it, and they would like to think that they might earn a living from working in the industry. However, as most readers will appreciate, their vision may be far too optimistic. The reality is that very few will become professional sports performers and the roads to becoming professional coaches, sports physiotherapists, psychologists or managers of leisure centres can be long and tortuous requiring high levels of dedication.

Generally, adults who have a wider experience of the world may have a clearer idea about the realities and will probably have made reasoned choices to seek qualifications that will enable them to work in the industry, changing direction in their career paths or enhancing their existing qualifications.

So what kinds of roles do our current portfolios of programmes prepare our learners for? SkillsActive is the sector skills council responsible for education and training in Sport and Leisure. Their website (www.skillsactive.com/training/ qualifications) gives a list of over 320 possible qualifications, and that does not include GCSEs and A levels. Table 1.3, overleaf, summarizes some of them but you would be well advised to visit this website yourselves for more details. Chapter 2 discusses the structure of these qualifications as defined by the Qualifications and Curriculum Development Agency (QCDA) in their Qualifications and Credit Framework (QCF) (www.qcda.gov.uk).

The main sectors of the industry

For our purposes, at this stage, we might note that Skills Active divides its work into five sub-sectors: Sport and Recreation, Health and Fitness, Outdoor Adventurous Activity, Play-work and Caravanning. Our concern in this publication is with the first three in particular, but you can see how difficult it is to apply strict definitions to the industry and perhaps how the interests of the various sub-sectors and, indeed, the interests of other industries such as Travel and Tourism, Hospitality and Retail might overlap. Provision of active leisure facilities might well be a major tourist attraction to some people; the adventure holiday sector has clear implications for the outdoor sub-sector and the customer service skills of the retail sector are clearly relevant to those aspects of Sport and Leisure that offer a service to the public.

Skills, knowledge and understanding for the Sport and Leisure industry

What kinds of activities, then, can our learners expect to engage in when working in the industry? Clearly, from the foregoing discussion there will be a very wide variety of things they might do from playing professional sports, to coaching groups and individuals and teaching classes; lifeguarding in public swimming pools; managing leisure centres; treating sports injuries and leading groups in outdoor adventure pursuits. The list is seemingly endless and constantly changing as new activities emerge, technologies develop and public interest also changes. As we have already seen, one major factor in these developments in recent years has undoubtedly been the concern over personal health and fitness which has fuelled the growth of fitness centres and gymnasia, both public and private.

Let us just consider for a moment the number of job roles and commensurate knowledge and skills that are required to run a successful fitness club (Reflection 1.5).

Table 1.3 Some of the qualifications endorsed by SkillsActive

Sport and Recreation	Adventure Activities	Health and Fitness
NVQ in Sport, Recreation and Allied Occupations: Coaching, Teaching and Instructing	Award in Single Pitch Rock Climbing Supervision	NVQ in Instructing Exercise and Fitness
BTEC National Diploma in Sport	NVQ in Outdoor Programmes	Certificate in Advanced Fitness Instructing (Gym)
Higher National Diploma in Sport and Leisure Management	BTEC Diploma in Sailing and Water Sports	Award in Step Exercise to Music
BTEC Award in Event Support	Award in Mountain Leadership	Certificate in Teaching Mat iPlates
NVQ in Achieving Excellence in Sports Performance	Certificate in Working in the Outdoors	Certificate in Instructing Health Related Exercise to Children
Certificate for Teaching/Coaching Aquatics	Certificate in Personal Development for the Outdoor Industry.	
Certificate for Coaching Golf		Award in Studio Resistance Training
Certificate in Coaching Gymnastics	Award in Basic Expedition Leadership	Award in Group Exercise Cycling
Certificate in First Aid for Sport		
Certificate in Sports Massage Therapy	SVQ3 in Outdoor Programmes (Outdoor Education)	Certificate in Teaching Yoga
Certificate in Pool Plant Operations	Certificate in Coaching Paddle Sport	Certificate in Personal Training
NVQ in Sport, Recreation and Allied Occupations: Operational Services		Certificate in Fitness Industry Studies

Reflection 1.5

The fitness suite in a local leisure centre has all the usual exercise stations for rowing, jogging, cycling and fixed weight equipment. It also has a free-weight training area and an exercise room for group aerobic activity and yoga, etc.

List the range of job roles that you think might be required to run the suite efficiently.

From your reflections, what skills knowledge and understanding would your learners need to develop to fulfil these roles competently? Here are some suggestions categorized under the headings of the various areas of responsibility:

- *Business Management skills* – strategic planning, finance, marketing, customer service, managing human and physical resources, legal obligations.
- *Activity skills* – health and safety, knowledge of the human body, its limits and capabilities, the range and variety of exercise options, coaching and teaching for fitness.
- *Maintenance skills* – of premises and equipment.

This is only one small segment of the industry, so now consider some of the others. For each of the possible occupational environments listed in Table 1.3, consider the range of knowledge and skills required to provide a service to the public.

How, then, can we begin to prepare our learners to work in the industry? Perhaps we can begin by considering the common ground. What skills and knowledge might be transferable from one sub-sector to another?

We have already suggested that there is an overlap and relationship between occupational sectors such as travel and tourism and sport and leisure, and the same must surely be true within the Sport and Leisure industry itself. The basic business skills and knowledge of planning, marketing, customer service and so on that are required to run our hypothetical fitness suite and an adventure holiday company or even a professional football club, must be very similar. Expert knowledge of the human body is required by the step aerobics teacher, the sports coach and the physiotherapist. So we find that the basis of many of our Sport and Leisure programmes is actually very similar. In fact, the structure of the QCF, discussed earlier and later in Chapter 2, reflects this in its credit framework and our learners very quickly become aware of the wider implications of their chosen career pathway.

Reflection 1.6

With reference to Table 1.3, the table of qualifications, your own knowledge of the various aspects of the industry, and perhaps using the prompts in Reflection 1.5, what job roles do you think would be available in an Adventurous Outdoor Activity Centre; a local leisure centre; a private multisports club (including tennis, squash, cricket and golf)?

The organization of the industry

With so many activities available under the umbrella of sport and leisure, is there an organizational framework to support and monitor them? How is central government funding allocated? Surely, there does need to be some kind of central organization to co-ordinate them and to ensure that funding is allocated fairly. Our interest, of course, is in the bodies specifically responsible for education and training but it is important to understand how they relate to the overall organizational structure. Figure 1.3 presents a diagrammatic view of the organization.

Activities take place within one of the three sectors that are funded *publicly* through central or local government, *privately* through commercial enterprise, or *voluntarily* through amateur sports and activity organizations or other charities. For our purposes, it is helpful to know that there are occupational opportunities in each of the sectors, even in the voluntary sector. The Ramblers' Association, for example, is a multi-million pound charitable trust that needs experienced professionals to manage its affairs.

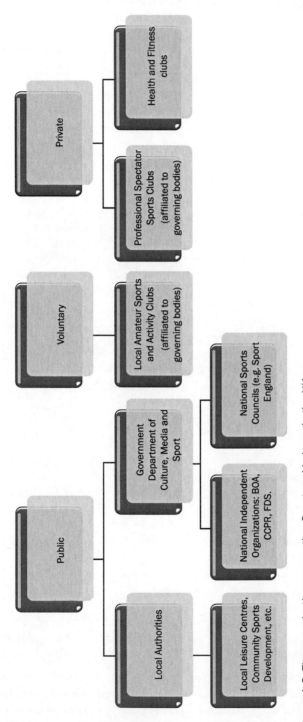

Figure 1.3 The organization supporting Sport and Leisure in the UK
Note that organizations such as the Central Council for Physical Recreation, the Confederation of British Sport and the British Olympic Association although partially funded by the National Government, are independent bodies.

The Youth Sport Trust and the Duke of Edinburgh's Award support the development of sport and Outdoor Adventure Activity through education, and there are a number of organizations that support social inclusion such as the Federation of Disability Sports, Sporting Equals (promoting racial equality in sport) and the Women's Sport and Fitness Foundation.

Funding of national sports projects

Sport in each of the home countries of the UK is governed by National Sports Councils which invest National Lottery and government funding in other organizations (such as sports governing bodies) and projects that will create opportunities for people to participate and excel in sport. They are accountable to the Department for Culture, Media and Sport through whom funding is channelled. UK sport also is funded by the government to promote elite, world-class performance.

All local and regional organizations will generally need to operate under the auspices of a governing body whether in the public, private or voluntary sector and within each of these, there may be opportunities for vocational development and training.

Organizations responsible for training and education in sport and leisure

Sector Skills Councils – SkillsActive
In 2002, the government launched an initiative which saw the creation of Sector Skills Councils (SSCs) who, as state-sponsored, employer-led organizations became responsible for training programmes in each occupational sector. In the case of sport and leisure, it was 'SkillsActive'. We have already considered the scope of their activities, suffice it to say that this organization is involved in all education and training related to the industry, co-ordinating the range of qualifications and giving its approval to any new ones.

Professional bodies – ISPAL and ISRM
There are, however, also two major professional bodies with a long history that deliver training programmes of their own generally related to organizational and administrative aspects of the industry: the Institute for Sport, Parks and Leisure (ISPAL) and the Institute of Sport and Recreation Management (ISRM). Both organizations play an important role in developing specialist training programmes for practitioners in management in sports and leisure training programmes which, nevertheless, generally fall within the nationally accredited framework.

Qualifications and Curriculum Development Agency (QCDA)
The body responsible for accrediting all programmes that would be eligible for government funding is the QCDA. We will describe their work in more detail in Chapter 2, but it is important to acknowledge at this stage that this is the organization appointed by government to co-ordinate and validate all qualifications that fall within the National Qualifications Credit Framework and to oversee their examination.

Teaching and learning for the Sport and Leisure industry

Clearly, knowledge of working practices and, indeed, an understanding of how people, both those who work within it and their clients, view the industry, must be the main driver for any vocational teaching and learning programmes. We shall be visiting some of these in Chapter 2, but to generalize, some train people in the skills and knowledge we have considered above, and others teach the underpinning principles of the industry. However, the practice of teaching and learning does not take place in isolation. We have already seen that a vast number of stakeholders are involved in our sector, and education is constantly under scrutiny from the public in general and from the government. As Paulo Freire observed, '[E]ducation is a political act' (1970: 67).

What we teach and the way that we teach are undoubtedly influenced by these 'stakeholders'. Thus we will review policies and initiatives that have had an impact on the teaching of Sport and Leisure, on educational practices and on the nature of those who may be our learners.

Government policy and national initiatives

Undoubtedly, next to the learners, the government, as the main funding body for education and training through the Department for Children, Families and Schools (DCFS), and the Department for Business Innovation and Skills (BIS), has to be a major stakeholder with an interest in developing knowledge, understanding and skills for the industry. Thus they will have the dominant influence in shaping the vocational curriculum largely through a range of policy statements and White Papers passed on to the educational community through Parliament.

The involvement of government in vocational education and training does, of course, date back at least to the beginning of the twentieth century. However, the origins of the current policies can be traced back to the 1980s and the beginnings of a New Vocationalism arising out of a reaction against what was perceived as the failure of the liberal education of the 1950s and 1960s to prepare young people with the skills for employment. Consequently, the 1980s saw a plethora of initiatives designed to address what was seen as a shortfall in employable skills. It is not within the remit of this publication to examine these in detail, and more can be found in other publications such as *Teaching and Training in Post-Compulsory Education* by Armitage et al. (2007). However, it is important to note that the new initiatives are not purely a phenomenon of the twenty-first century.

Yet even at the beginning of the twenty-first century there has been a whole raft of initiatives, reports and White Papers affecting the development of vocational education and training, all of which are important, but we will highlight those that seem to be immediately relevant to our case.

Each of these initiatives has had considerable impact on the opportunities for learners (and thus the profiles of learning groups) and on the structure of the curriculum, so it is worth spending a few moments considering them.

Reflection 1.7

What do you know about the following?

- 14–19 Opportunity and Excellence
- The Tomlinson Report: 14–19 curriculum and qualifications reform
- 14–19 Education and Skills White Paper

- Young Apprenticeships
- Modern Apprenticeships
- The Leitch Report
- Every Child (Learner) Matters

14–19 Opportunity and Excellence (2003)

This policy document addressed the agenda for a more coherent programme for 14–19 learners and outlined many initiatives that would transform the provision of education for this phase. For our purposes, the main ones were: providing opportunities for entry to employment, including Modern Apprenticeships and pre-vocational programmes; the stimulation of collaboration between educational establishments and work-based training providers; providing financial support through the EMA (Educational Maintenance Allowance); offering a much stronger vocational programme with a firm underpinning of general education and developing a unified framework of qualifications suitable for all young people of all abilities.

The Tomlinson Report (2004)

It was as a result of this last proposal that a working group chaired by Mike Tomlinson was charged to advise the government on the long-term 'shape of reforms'. The final report was published in October 2004, proposing sweeping changes to the whole education programme for the 14–19 phase that would indeed have provided a coherent, 'unified framework' of qualifications. Unfortunately, this appeared to be too drastic a solution and the eventual model which was based on the group's proposals focused largely on the vocational education elements and were reincarnated as the new 14–19 Diplomas, a mere shadow of Mike Tomlinson's vision.

14–19 Education and Skills White Paper (2005)

Setting out the general agenda for the development of 14–19 education and skills, this White Paper addressed a number of issues from the modification of A/AS levels to the introduction of Functional Skills and the new 'specialized' Diplomas, as we have seen above, modelled on the Tomlinson recommendations with significant input from employers through the relevant Sector Skills Councils (see earlier). From the point of view of this publication, these two points are important since they will have an impact on how we teach our programmes of Sport and Leisure: Functional Skills are to be embedded into the curriculum and the pedagogical emphasis on vocational education programmes will, naturally enough, be on experiential and applied learning. For more information, see www.literacytrust.org.uk/socialinclusion/youngpeople/1419paper.

Young Apprenticeships

Launched in September 2004, the Young Apprenticeships scheme enabled learners at Key Stage 4 in partnership with schools, colleges and employers to take vocational qualifications. They spend three days at school following their normal academic studies and two days on the YA programme. The teacher of Sport and Leisure may well be involved with these learners since apart from structured work experience, they take a level 2 qualification such as a National Diploma and an NVQ level in Sport and Recreation. For more information, see www.skillsactive.com/training/apprenticeships/young-apprenticeships.

Modern Apprenticeships and Advanced Apprenticeships (2001)

Apprentices are full-time employees, doing a normal job 'building up knowledge and skills, gaining qualifications and earning money at the same time' and could be any age over 16. They will probably be working towards a work-based qualification such as an NVQ and may be elite athletes, contracted youth players in professional club academies, leisure and sports assistants, coaches and instructors, among many others. As a teacher, you might be responsible for managing the training and, particularly, assessing the development of these learners: in which case, you would need to be qualified at NVQ level 3 Assessor's award (A1 or A2). For more information, see www.apprenticeships.org.uk.

The Leitch Report (2006)

Lord Sandy Leitch's report has at least stimulated much debate in the post-16 educational sector. Commissioned to review the state of the nation's skills needs, thought to be well below international standards, his recommendations placed responsibility for skills training largely in the hands of employers. Ninety-five per cent of adults are expected to achieve basic skills levels in functional literacy and numeracy and 90 per cent should be qualified at least to level 2 in occupational skills. Additional funding is recommended to be routed through 'Train to Gain' schemes which provide funding for employers to provide training opportunities for their employees in collaboration with colleges and private training providers. Your adult learners will, quite possibly, be those released by employers under this scheme. For more information, see www.dcsf.gov.uk/furthereducation.

Every Child (Learner) Matters (ECM)

We shall be reviewing the ECM agenda later in Chapter 4 in the context of learning and teaching, but it is a government initiative that has had considerable impact on the way in which learning is managed in schools and colleges. Embedded in the Children Act (2004), its main purpose is to promote the development of each child or learner through the following principles:

- to be healthy
- to stay safe
- to enjoy and achieve
- to make a positive contribution
- to achieve economic well-being.

It expected that every teacher will plan to integrate these principles into every lesson where possible (Donovan 2005: 18–26).

The life experiences and aspirations of different groups of learners

Generalizations should come with a cautionary note: people are different and don't fit neatly into the categories we devise for them and, in any case, there is a danger that we might be led into stereotyping them and leading them in turn into the 'self-fulfilling prophesy' trap where they will behave in the manner expected of them according to the teacher's perceptions (Hargreaves et al. 1975).

Hyland and Merrill are clear that colleges of FE in particular are 'cosmopolitan institutions' that 'cater for everyone, 16–19 year olds, both academic and vocational, adult returners, access students, HE students, those with special needs, the socially excluded and those not involved anywhere else' (Green and Lucas 1999: 35, cited in Hyland and Merrill 2003: 47).

Schools too have now developed much broader curricula to include not only the traditional GCSE and A level routes, but also applied learning programmes such as National Diplomas and the new Diplomas.

Clearly, the 14+ Lifelong Learning Sector must include a wide range of learners from young adults with perhaps inflated aspirations, to more mature students of Sport and Leisure who might be returning to work and/or study, seeking promotion through further professional development or perhaps a change in direction in their careers. What can we, as teachers, expect them to bring to the classroom and what do they expect from us? Here we try to identify their ambitions and needs so that we can create learning activities that will help them to achieve those aspirations.

Reflection 1.8

Look at Box 1.1, overleaf. What advice would you give Sarah in terms of pursuing a career in SAL?

Aspirations of young adults

Our younger learners in this sector will be found largely in schools and in colleges of Further Education, although some may well be engaged in new apprenticeship programmes, and thus in full-time employment. We consider these programmes in detail in Chapter 2, so it is sufficient at this stage to say that the programmes they will most likely be engaged in will be the New Diplomas, National Diplomas and Certificates, and NVQs.

All young people at the age of 14 will have experienced sport and leisure as a part of the compulsory National Curriculum through their Physical Education (PE) lessons. They will, then, at least have a good idea of a range of sports, fitness and possibly adventurous outdoor activities, and for many these experiences may well have been highly enjoyable because of the success they might have achieved and the enthusiasm of their PE teachers. Undoubtedly, their view of these experiences may also have been modified by the influence of a media which tends to glamorize the lives of the superstars. Experience shows us that many enrol on Sports and Leisure vocational programmes attracted by the notion that their studies will involve

Box 1.1 Case study BTEC National Sport and Exercise Sciences learner

Sarah is a 19-year-old learner on the first year of a two-year BTEC Level 3 Extended Diploma in Sport and Exercise Science. She says:

> It basically came down to two choices, I could stay at school and do A Levels and go to university or I could go to the college and study on this course, and still go to university if I chose to. I guess I chose the course because it meant that I could study sport and exercise in more depth and not have to worry about taking A level choices that I didn't really want to take, other than PE. This way, I get to study stuff that interests me, I have no exams but still work really hard, but I get to enjoy the whole week. I am not sure exactly what I want to do at the end, I am hoping that my second year Work-Based Experience unit will help me decide, but I don't feel any pressure to decide at this stage. My tutors are all sports or fitness people and have worked in a number of exciting places, one of them was a high level coach and I think this may be a career option for me as I am an elite squash player and have already been asked by the region to do some coaching.

engagement in active sports most of the time. The realities of understanding underpinning theory or the mundane nature of much of the work that supports the industry has somehow eluded them.

Of course, this is not to deny that there are also many who have a really genuine interest in pursuing a professional career as a coach or sports physiotherapist, for example, and who choose to follow a path which might lead to university.

Behavioural issues of the younger adult

So can we generalize about the characteristics and aspirations of these young people in a way that is helpful to developing programmes of learning that are meaningful to them, or do differences for each learner make such generalizations meaningless? Educationists, psychologists and sociologists have attempted to identify general characteristics of young learners which we perhaps ought to consider when designing our learning and teaching programmes.

From time to time, critics of the education system in the media, at governmental level, or even from within the educational community itself, have been critical of the education system as it has been seen to be failing many young people. Donovan (2005: 9) points to DfES statistics to support the view that there is a strong correlation 'between poor attendance and behaviour at school and later anti-social behaviour and criminality'.

Why are so many disaffected and 'failing'? Lumby and Foskett (2005: 77) point to a study of secondary school learners by Thomas et al. (2000) in which, '48 per cent found school always or sometimes boring, 21 per cent felt teachers never or hardly ever listened and . . . 25 per cent of 16-year-olds felt the worst thing about school was problems with particular lessons'.

Modern life does perhaps present our young learners (and indeed mature adults!) with a whole set of bewildering problems, not least the very pace of life itself and the changes this brings. In 1976, Horrocks identified six 'points of reference' in viewing adolescence, but these still have validity today. It is a time when young people become more aware of an 'idealised self' and of physical development and 'body image'; a time of seeking status both as an individual and within a social group; and it is a time of intellectual expansion and evaluation of ideas (Horrocks 1976, cited in Harkin et al. 2001: 56).

Thus we are confronted by a range of emotions and ambitions in the Sport and Leisure classroom. The notion of the 'teenager' is a concept dating back to the 1940s (Savage 2008). It is a concept that has generated the creation of a youth culture which undoubtedly brings with it anticipated behaviours and expectations. So the abiding feature of the teenage years, and perhaps the most important aspect for us in planning a programme of learning, is the seeking out and establishing of an identity for the maturing adult: supporting the 'rite of passage' to an adult life of responsibility.

For our young adult who specifically wishes to study a programme of Sport and Leisure, this is their chosen route to a vocational identity: a place in the working environment of their social world, a world that is constantly and rapidly changing against a background of media and peer pressure and the ready availability of the vestiges of adult life such as 'leisure drugs', alcohol and recreational sex.

The potential to motivate the younger learner

We have suggested above that one major contributory cause of lack of learner engagement and disaffection has been a lack of 'meaningfulness' of the subject and the manner in which it has been presented. Thus, extrapolating the forgoing argument, planning to teach vocational programmes such as Sport and Leisure offers the distinct possibility of developing environments that at least offer the chance of 'meaningful learning' simply because they might be seen as being situated in the young learner's world of reality.

Given all these changes and developments, it is no wonder that young people in the classroom appear to behave in ways that will assert their individuality of body and mind. Chapter 4 will propose that there are ways to facilitate individual learning and to channel intellectual, social and emotional development to enhance learning.

At the same time, we should be wary of relying that a presumed interest in the subject itself is enough to command engagement. We must also be aware that, for many, continuing education at 16 plus is merely a more attractive alternative to work and that a subject such as Sport and Leisure conjures up particularly attractive images. Of course, the Education and Skills Act, 2008, based on the Green Paper, *Raising Expectations* (2007) will mean that all young people up to the age of 18 will soon compulsorily have to engage in some form of education and training, so developing the meaningful curriculum will become an even more urgent imperative.

Reflection 1.9

Look at Box 1.2. What factors would you take into consideration when preparing a learning programme for John?

Box 1.2 Case study of an adult learner

John's day-time job (and sometimes night-shift) is as driver on the London Underground. He trains regularly at a local fitness gym and has been attending evening classes at a local college where he has successfully studied level 2 Anatomy and Physiology and now is working towards an NVQ in Teaching, Coaching and Instructing (Gymnasium) with ambitions to become an instructor or even a Personal Fitness Advisor at least part-time.

Mature adults

Why then would a mature adult wish to study Sport and Leisure? Bearing in mind our previous comments about making generalizations, we would, nevertheless, suggest that there are four main groups of mature learners to consider.

The first, and probably the largest group, will be those who are keen participants and want to contribute to the growth of their chosen sport(s) by gaining a coaching or instructing award, like John in our case study. Among these will be parents of young sports people, sports men and women retiring from higher levels of performance or perhaps people who have only ever wanted to coach. But, be sure, they will be committed to their ambition.

The second is the group who, having completed programmes at level 3 (A levels, National Diplomas and perhaps NVQs), want to continue their studies in greater depth in Higher Education at a university or even at a college of Further Education. These will generally fall within the age group of 19 to 25 years old.

The third group consists of learners probably, but not necessarily, from about 23 years old onwards, who, having opted out of education post-16 to start work or perhaps through family commitments, now wish to return to their studies. Undoubtedly, a number of these will have come from the group of disaffected learners discussed above: learners who, as more mature adults, have developed an identity that they feel they can develop through a career in Sport and Leisure. They might be engaged in any of the programmes considered in Chapter 2 at any level, but most likely those from level 2 onwards.

Finally, there will be those learners already employed in the industry seeking to develop their skills and knowledge through a programme of Continuing Professional Development (CPD). This group might include people involved in other career paths who are looking for a change in direction (we did suggest some related careers earlier). Their focus will probably be on higher level programmes with specific professional outcomes, such as the level 4 ISRM/City and Guilds Higher Professional

Diploma in Supervisory Management which will enable them to aspire to Leisure Centre Management, or the ISPA level 3 Certificate in Community Sports Work (see earlier sections on ISRM and ISPA).

The particular profiles of these learners can be identified through their descriptions: some will have in-depth experience of the industry already, while others may have virtually none apart from regular participation in sports activity or visits to the gym. However, almost certainly, they will all have one thing in common: because they have chosen to take this course of study, often against the odds and at personal cost, they will be highly motivated. Furthermore, most of them will have had experience of the world of work or at least of the rigours of adult life.

Clearly, all this has implications for the approach that we might take with mature adults, as opposed to how we might plan to teach younger students of Sport and Leisure who are either still a part of the compulsory education phase, or within two or three years of this. We will consider this in more detail in Chapter 4.

Summary

In this chapter we have attempted to present an overview of Sport and Leisure as a curriculum area. To many non-specialists it might appear to be a subject lacking in depth: we hope that this chapter will help to allay those perceptions and give those dedicated to its promotion information to convince their doubters.

We have considered the contribution it makes to the nation as a whole in terms of the economy and to the development of society, but also its potential as an activity to give meaning to and change people's lives. Clearly, the wide range of activities available in the sector creates opportunities to satisfy all types of individual needs and this, in turn, creates opportunities for careers. We have considered the range of skills, knowledge and understanding needed to service the industry, the organizations that provide opportunities for education and training, and the government initiatives that have supported their activities. Finally, we have tried to analyse the nature of the learners that we can expect to find in our classes.

Our aim has been to provide a background to the learning and teaching environment which will inform the way in which we deliver our learning programmes in Sport and Leisure, which is the main object of this publication.

But what of the future? At the time of writing, there are the possibilities of major changes in the political scene, and undoubtedly this will have implications for learning and teaching. We hope that this publication will be sufficiently generic to be adaptable for any curriculum developments. One such change that we have had to address in writing this is that driven by government health policies, there has been a change in emphasis away from pure anatomy and physiology towards applied studies in health and fitness such as fitness testing and programmes.

Our next chapter, then, will look at the context of curriculum development through the programmes in Sport and Leisure.

2

Developing the Sport and Leisure curriculum

In this chapter we will be looking at:

- The notion of 'curriculum'
- Curriculum theory and practice in the context of Sport and Leisure programmes
- The national structure of qualifications in the UK
- The range of programmes and qualifications
- How to plan a scheme of work

Introduction: what is a curriculum?

'Programmes' of Sport and Leisure studies really provide us with the structure for our curriculum. But what do we mean by 'curriculum'? This chapter aims to unravel some of the mysteries of the notion and to examine the theory behind the many programmes that make up the Sport and Leisure curriculum.

Reflection 2.1

Think about your own most recent experience as a learner. What subject(s) were you studying?

What else did you learn while on this course?

What was your 'curriculum'? What do you think we mean by the 'curriculum'?

One key educationist was Lawrence Stenhouse, who, although writing in 1975, has had considerable impact on the development of our concepts of curriculum. He began by referring to the definition of curriculum in the *Shorter Oxford English Dictionary*: 'a course: especially a regular course of study as at a school or university' (Stenhouse 1975: 1). This is derived from the Latin which referred to running a course. In this case, curriculum might be described as 'the planned intentions of government and of teachers/trainers in their organisations' (Armitage et al. 2007: 180). This would appear to focus on the content of the curriculum.

However, Stenhouse really considers that there is more to it than this. He points us to the 'reality of teaching and learning for teachers and students' (Armitage et al. 2007: 180). In other words, it is the totality of the learning experience which would include factors such as the general aims of the institution: is its primary aim to prepare people for university education or for an occupational role? Is there a focus on citizenship, preparing people for a 'useful' role in society? It would also include the teachers' priorities: do they see themselves as mere purveyors of knowledge, or do they want their learners to develop as autonomous learners who can organize their own learning? Although, as we shall see, these notions are not always obvious, they undoubtedly do have an impact on the curriculum and, therefore, are often referred to as the 'hidden curriculum'. So, Stenhouse was arguing that the study of curriculum is important because we should 'examine [the] balance between intentions and realities and use this information to improve [our] work and enhance students' learning' (Armitage et al. 2007: 181).

Tony Nasta (1994) helps us a little here when he makes a distinction between a 'course' and a 'programme'. In his view, a course 'reflects the traditional world of vocational education . . . The pedagogical model is paramount, namely that there is a recognised body of knowledge which has to be imparted.' However, a 'learning programme challenges all these conventions . . . It is the integration of knowledge and skills . . . [in which] learning becomes a partnership between the teacher as facilitator and the student.' You will find that we generally talk about 'programmes' rather than 'course' in this publication. This is because we believe that the curriculum is about the totality of the learning experience.

Reflection 2.2

Now reconsider the definition that you came up with in Reflection 2.1 in the light of the above.

Think about a particular 'course' that you have undertaken at any time in your career and try to analyse what your teacher(s) were aiming to achieve in terms of your own development.

Has your perception of 'curriculum' changed at all? If so, in what way?

Behind all this discussion, then, there is a deeper meaning that can help us, perhaps, to understand the development of our Sport and Leisure programmes and why there are so many different types, and also to compare and contrast them.

Curriculum ideologies and Sport and Leisure programmes

The first and most obvious starting point is to say that Sport and Leisure is a working industry and that people who want to be employed in it need to acquire certain specific skills. A programme that just trains people for these skills (programmes such as NVQs, for example) is known as instrumentalist. This is a view that currently seems to dominate educational policy today as we saw in Chapter 1 where we referred to the 'New Vocationalism', or the overwhelming desire to improve the nation's skills base.

But what of the knowledge and understanding that underpin and inform this practice? Surely the gym instructor needs to have a good understanding of human anatomy and physiology? And wouldn't the sports coach benefit from understanding the psychology of his athlete? Perhaps the leisure centre manager would provide a better service if she had some idea of the social needs of her community? Programmes that focus on knowledge and understanding would be called 'academic'. This is a view that is known as 'Classical Humanism' since its roots go back as far as the ancient Greeks who believed that progress was determined by the growth of human knowledge, although, as we have seen before, this tended to be limited to the ruling elite.

However, there are many educationists who would be very critical of both of these types of programme because they are very limited in how they address wider educational aims. How do they prepare people to become independent, autonomous learners who can take responsibility for their own learning, for example? Such educationists, influenced by theorists and philosophers such as John Dewey (1859–1952) and Carl Rogers (1902–87), set about designing a different type of curriculum which is known as 'Progressivist-Humanist'. This is because they are 'learner-centred' and focus not so much on the subject matter but on developing the study skills of learners by encouraging them to think for themselves and to question assumptions about the subject of study, in our case, Sport and Leisure. The teacher would then facilitate and guide their research to help them in their studies, thus enabling them to develop as 'autonomous learners', a theme that I hope you will find repeated often throughout this publication.

These different 'ideologies', or beliefs about the purpose of education, lead to certain styles of teaching and types, or models, of curriculum. First, there is the 'product' model that focuses on the *outcomes* of the programme (what can the learner do as a result of the experience?). Then there is the 'content' model, which focuses on *what* is learnt, and, finally, the 'process' model, which focuses on *how* people learn.

There is not space in this publication to explore this fascinating world of ideologies and curriculum models further, but there is ample literature on it and a good starting point would be *Teaching and Training in Post-Compulsory Education* by Andy Armitage et al. (2007).

As implied earlier, this is important when studying the various curriculum alternatives in Sport and Leisure programmes since they serve different purposes and have different ideologies that drive them.

Reflection 2.3

From what you know about each of the following and from considering the above, which ideology would best describe these programmes? Why do think that?

- National Diploma in Sport Science.
- A level Sport Studies.
- NVQ in Teaching, Coaching and Instructing (Gym).
- Pool Lifeguard.

To help you, start by thinking about what their main purpose is. For example, is it to gain a specific qualification so that your learners can be employed in a leisure centre? Or, will it give them UCCAS points so that they can go to university?

You will probably have realized that most programmes have elements of a number, if not all of these ideologies and models. So how does this help us understand the pedagogy of our subject? That is, how do we teach Sport and Leisure or facilitate its learning?

The ideology and pedagogy of the Sport and Leisure curriculum

The manner of our teaching/facilitating will be influenced by the type of programme, the content of the curriculum, our students' preferred learning styles and, indeed, by our own beliefs (or ideology) about education. For example, if we believe that the learners just need to know how to safely manage equipment in a gym, then our lessons may just consist of learning how to use it safely, almost mechanically. On the other hand, if we want our learners to consider the physical, psychological and social impact of sporting activity on individuals, then we might lecture them on these factors and then set research projects for them to study one or two in some depth independently.

In order to develop our understanding of how we ought to promote learning on these programmes, it will be useful to know what they are and what they aim to provide for our learners.

The origins of Sport and Leisure programmes

We have already noted how, in the UK, Physical Education (PE) became a curriculum subject and developed from the late nineteenth century through the whole of the twentieth. But its focus as a subject until about the 1960s was always on physical activity, on exercise for health and the development of skills in sport. However, from this time on, the focus began to shift: PE professionals, perhaps wanting to raise the status of their subject, lobbied to make it an examinable subject and the CSE in PE was born. This later developed into GCSE, of course, and from the mid-1970s onwards the movement gathered momentum spurred on by the growth in public interest in participation in sport and leisure and post-war investment in local leisure centres.

So the movement inspired the development not only of personal engagement with sport and leisure programmes, but also of programmes that might prepare people to staff the leisure centres and pursue a vocation in this growing industry. At first there was a lack of qualifications that fitted the requirements of the industry. Thus, a number of PE teachers and lecturers, particularly in colleges of FE began to write their own programmes and to promote Leisure as a vocational subject. To validate their programmes they worked with examining bodies such as City and Guilds (C&G) and the Business and Technology Education Council (BTEC) and so C&G481 leading to careers in Leisure Management, and BTEC Nationals in Sport and Leisure were born.

Throughout the 1980s the number of courses, qualifications and indeed students on these programmes grew, and other strands of qualifications began to be developed. On the one hand, there were the strictly vocational qualifications, spawned by a burgeoning instrumentalist ideology that we mentioned earlier, and, on the other, an 'academic' strand, promoted by educationists desirous of seeing the subject developed and studied in depth. Thus, the instrumentalist agenda was represented by NVQs (National Vocational Qualifications) and the academic by A levels in Sport Studies and PE. Instrumentalism tends to lead to a 'product'-driven curriculum: at the end of the programme the learners would have the skills to make them employable in the industry. A levels were more 'content'-driven: certain knowledge and understanding were promoted so that students might qualify for university where they might engage in an academic study of sport such as Sport Science. But, alongside these programmes, BTEC were developing National Diplomas in Sport and Leisure which generally had a work-related focus. This is important to this story because they were developing a different philosophy to the delivery and assessment of their qualifications. This was a more 'process'-driven curriculum, focusing on the development of study skills, learning how to learn, through research assignment activities.

Clearly, such different ideologies have implications for the pedagogy (how we teach) of our subject. Morrison and Ridley (1989) provide a very clear model (Table 2.1) which, in summary, identifies how the ideology will influence the manner of delivery, the relationship between the teacher and learner, the way in which the programme will be assessed and the types of resources used. The latter two will be discussed in Chapters 5 and 6 respectively, but you might like to consider how this might be applied in Reflection 2.4.

Reflection 2.4

With reference to Table 2.1, which summarizes Morrison and Ridley's notion of 'pedagogical theories', complete the chart in Table 2.2 for teaching each of the following:

1   Anatomy – naming the components and bones of the human skeleton and analysing their function.
2   How to organize a coaching session for a community sports leaders' session.
3   How to research and analyse the cultural mix of users in a local leisure centre.

We might hope that you will have identified the largely 'classical humanist' nature of (1) which asks the learners to engage in cognitive activity; the instrumentalist philosophy of (2) which focuses on practical application; and the Humanist approach in (3) where the learners are engaging in process-based skills that will develop them as autonomous learners.

Table 2.1 How ideologies can influence the way in which a curriculum is delivered

	Progressivism/ learner-centred	Classical Humanism/ academic	Instrumentalism
Emphasis	The individual learner	The acquisition of knowledge	The acquisition of skill
Theory of knowledge	Emphasis on the process of learning	Development of subject disciplines	Development of 'useful' knowledge and skills
Theory of learning and the learner's role	Experiential learning: development of learner autonomy	Obedience, passivity – accepting the teacher as the font of knowledge	Induction into vocationally relevant areas
Theory of teaching and the teacher's role	The teacher as facilitator of learning – guiding the learner towards autonomy	Instructor, information transmitter, authoritative formal tutor	Instructor, trainer transmitter of vocationally relevant experience
Assessment	Diagnostic, multiple criteria, informal profiling – fulfilling learner potential	Written, formal, attainment testing, examinations	Formal, written and oral (e.g. Key Skills), practical
Resources	First-hand (from experience) and diverse	Second-hand (from text-books, etc.) and restricted	Narrowly relevant to the content, practical vocational

Source: Adapted from Morrison and Ridley, in Preedy (1989: 50).

Table 2.2 Interpreting Morrison and Ridley's theory

	Naming the bones of the human skeleton	How to organize a community sports coaching session	Analysing data from a research project
Main focus – the learner, content or outcomes?			
What knowledge is developed? Process, product or subject matter?			
What is the learner's role?			
What is the teacher's role?			
How is it assessed?			
What types of resources are required?			

However, you may disagree with our analysis and might have found this exercise difficult because each example is perhaps ambiguous. In fact, what we generally find is that our curricula rarely fall totally within one particular school of thought, or ideology. More often than not, there are aspects of each present, and identification is more a question of emphasis where one ideology dominates. For example, all our programmes will have objectives, or some kind of outcome in mind, even if this relates to the processes of learning rather than the development of a specific skill or knowledge set, so, arguably, there is always a 'product' in mind.

Bearing this in mind, then, we shall consider the range of programmes that you might find in schools and colleges today and you might like to reflect on the underpinning ideologies of each.

Range of programmes

Levels and the NQF

To understand the context of these programmes you will need to also understand the overarching structure of the qualifications framework. We briefly mentioned the role of the Qualifications and Curriculum Development Agency (QCDA) in Chapter 1. It is their responsibility to review and monitor all qualifications offered by awarding bodies and to demonstrate how they fit into the framework: generally, programmes outside of this will not be able to attract government funding. Currently, the framework is undergoing a major modification, changing from a National Qualification Framework (NQF) to a Qualifications and Credit Framework (QCF) to be launched in September 2010. The implication is that, in future, it will be possible for learners to gain credits from a variety of learning programmes, further enabling them to design their own programmes, but for our purposes, to help understand the concept of levels, in Table 2.3 we illustrate some qualifications as they appeared in the NQF.

Under the new QCF, qualifications are made up of units that allocate credits as opposed to guided learning hours, and qualifications will be sized in terms of the number of credits that they generate.

Programme specifications, validated by QCDA, are provided by the three main awarding bodies, AQA, Edexcel and OCR: they can be downloaded by visiting their websites which are found in the bibliography.

Table 2.3 The National Qualifications Framework (adapted)

Levels	Qualifications	
Level 4	HND	Foundation degree
Level 3	National Diploma	A Levels
Level 2	First Diploma	GCSE a–c
Level 1	Foundation Diploma	GCSE d–g

Box 2.1 Case study mix and match qualifications

Under the new credit system, a training provider can mix and match qualifications provided that the majority of the credits are achieved from an existing stand-alone qualification.

Bethany studies on a BTEC level 3 Diploma in Sport that incorporates a coaching qualification, a First Aid course and a level 1 Fitness Instructors course.

She will accumulate credits for each of these: what are the advantages for her in developing a career path? What is the range of environments in which she might be employable?

GCSE

At levels 1 to 2, GCSE PE provides a sound foundation for many young learners to begin to acquire the knowledge and understanding required to underpin higher level programmes. The focus is very much on the development of healthy lifestyles through physical activity, including a basic understanding of anatomy and physiology. However, learners are also required to understand the historical and socio-cultural contexts of sport, thus setting the tone for this interdisciplinary subject. Most importantly the GCSE provides young learners, who are talented in sports activity, or perhaps just interested in it, with the opportunity to achieve a qualification in a subject with which they can fully engage. It is assessed by both practical tests and by examination.

AS and A level

AS and A level PE are level 3 qualifications that offer the opportunity for learners to study the subject in greater depth. 'The focus is on participation and performance in physical activity as part of a balanced, active and healthy lifestyle' (OCR 2008). So, the learner is required to study their own performance in the context of a broad spectrum of disciplines, such as we noted for GCSE: anatomy and physiology, biomechanics, history, psychology and socio-cultural aspects. Indeed, this might be the first truly interdisciplinary curriculum. Although there is a 'Classical Humanist', knowledge-based agenda here which is assessed in the appropriate manner by written examination, there is also a strong element of applied studies in which learners monitor and analyse performance and fitness, developing a deeper understanding of the nature of sports performance through learner-centred study of the more Progressive-Humanist kind.

National Diplomas and certificates

National diplomas in Sport and Sport Science are now offered at levels two and three by the Edexcel and OCR exam boards, whose roles we discuss in Chapter 5.

However, as we have seen, they have their origins in the BTEC diplomas of the 1980s and developed a very distinct characteristic of their own as a process-driven, learner-centred programme with a focus on work-related learning. The popularity of these programmes among teachers, particularly in colleges of Further Education, is such that they have survived many threats to their existence, notably the introduction of the GNVQ qualifications in the 1990s, so that they are now firmly embedded in the qualifications framework. Although they include assignments that are externally set and examined, most assignments are set and assessed by the teachers who deliver the programmes, thus allowing some measure of autonomy and the possibility of structuring them to fulfil their own learners' needs, which might be related, for example, to the opportunities presented by the local environment. As we shall see in Chapter 5, standards are maintained through the application of rigorous external moderation.

The New Diplomas

The New Diplomas are the outcome of the Tomlinson Report of 2004 on the future of post-14 education in the UK, although, as we noted in Chapter 1, they are really but a shadow of his vision. Mike Tomlinson and his team were charged with suggesting ways in which all young learners from 14–19-years-old might become better engaged with an education system that promoted equity between academic and vocational programmes. They concluded that the only way was to completely change the structure of the system and proposed a 'unified system of diplomas' which would mean replacing A levels and GCSEs.

> It is our view that the status quo is not an option. Nor do we believe further piecemeal changes are desirable . . .

> Our report sets out a clear vision for a unified framework of 14–19 curriculum and qualifications.
>
> (Working Group on 14–19 Reform 2004: 1)

Unfortunately, established views are perhaps too deeply entrenched for such radical change, so we are left with a model that is somewhat less than that envisaged.

Table 2.4 presents a summary of the structure of the New Diplomas as they are

Table 2.4 Structure of the New Diplomas

Principle learning	Generic learning	Additional and/or specialist learning
Mandatory Units	Functional skills:	Complementary learning, adding breadth or depth
The number varies according to the level and the learning line	English, maths, ICT	
	Personal, learning and thinking skills	Progression pathways
Sector-related		Choice
50% applied learning	Work experience (min. 10 days) project	

available now. In principle, they offer a holistic curriculum for every learner and to an extent do enshrine the Tomlinson view of a diploma that included not only elements of vocational education, but also prepared learners for a role in the wider world through a programme of 'generic learning'. This includes the development of Functional Skills, which would contextualize Maths, English and ICT into their life worlds and also of Personal Learning and Thinking Skills which would prepare them for a more fulfilling role in society in general and in the workplace in particular. Chapter 3 deals with these in greater depth.

Again, the specifications are available on exam boards' websites, but you will see that they have followed a similar structure to that of the National and first Diplomas. Furthermore, there is also a substantial element of 'Personalized and Additional Learning' which is intended to give the learner scope to follow other interests of their own and perhaps gain additional qualifications such as A levels, First or National Diplomas or even those that will prepare them to actually start a job of work in their chosen field including NVQs or Pool-Lifeguarding awards.

Higher National Diplomas and Certificates (HNDs/HNCs) and Foundation Degrees

It may be that you will find yourself teaching in a college that is accredited to teach programmes at Higher Education Levels, in which case, you may teach on an HND in Sport and Exercise Sciences or Sport and Leisure Management, both of which are to be found in Edexcel's suite of qualifications. These programmes provide natural progression to Higher Education, especially for learners on National Diploma programmes. Again, the focus is generally work-related and the curriculum model is process-based, but the level of study is at level four on the qualifications framework (HE level 1) with opportunities to progress to level five (HE level 2) modules and further even to top up to an honours degree after a further year's study.

Both qualifications are supported by the professional bodies, and it is possible for candidates who successfully achieve the awards to become members of the British Association of Sport and Exercise Science (BASES) or the Institute of Sport and Recreation Management (ISRM).

In the spirit of extending the curriculum to challenge all learners, at the time of writing there have even been enquiries from schools with a view to developing an HND/C programme. So if your teaching environment is in schools, there may well be opportunities for you to extend your portfolio to begin teaching at HE levels.

National Vocational Qualifications (NVQs): the instrumentalist agenda manifest

In Chapter 1, we noted the development of the New Vocationalism in the 1980s, with an agenda to improve the nation's skills base in order to become more competitive in the global economy, and the role of NVQs as a part of that agenda. One of the objectives of the NVQ was to provide a unified, more coherent system of vocational qualifications. Whether this has been the case or not is open to debate and you must make up your own mind based on the evidence of your experience. However,

NVQs are currently the system in use and you will most likely come across groups and individuals who are engaged in developing portfolios of evidence to achieve their qualification.

In terms of our ideologies and models, they most definitely would be seen to be instrumentalist and product-based since they set out to ensure that the learners develop and provide evidence for the skills, knowledge and understanding to prove that they are competent in a specific job role. However, it is interesting to note that they are couched in a vocabulary that is often seemingly learner-centred and progressive.

The debate on 'competency-based assessment' (for that is what this is rather than learning) is prolific and it is worth spending a little time reading the varying points of view found in Hyland (1994), Wolf (2000) and Lea et al. (2003).

Nevertheless, many of our readers will either be working with groups that are developing their vocational skills through NVQs or may even have their appetite whetted enough by this discussion to add the odd NVQ to their own curriculum as a means of providing a qualification for their learners that is accepted by the industry as a sign of competence in the workplace. Bethany in Box 2.1 is a case in point. They could, indeed, complement other programmes such as National Diplomas or as Additional Specialist Learning in the New Diplomas, or could even be stand-alone programmes.

The range of NVQs available in Sport and Leisure is comprehensive and covers occupational activities from aspects of management, to gym instructing and sports coaching, to sports development. Again, a visit to the exam boards' websites will be well rewarded.

The National Open College Network (NOCN)

One of the most potent forces for change in adult education has been the development of NOCN. Yet, as NIACE observe in their document celebrating 25 years of the movement, it is one of the most closely guarded secrets in the history of education. Originally working mainly with adult returners, historically, it has been at the cutting edge of the credit-based framework and its programmes are validated by QCDA and therefore have currency within the qualifications system and also can draw down funding.

Box 2.2 gives a summary of NOCN mission and values from which you can clearly see the ethical underpinning of the organization as being committed to equal opportunities and enabling learners to achieve their potential through the recognition of their achievements via credit accumulation. That means recognizing the value of each stage of their learning.

In principle, NOCN programmes are designed by teachers for their specific groups of learners, and thus are, perhaps, the most learner-centred programmes of all. Teachers can write their own units which are rigorously scrutinized by the regional panels. We can personally vouch for the rigour from experience both as a programme reviewer and as having been reviewed! Approved modules then enter the national database and may be drawn down to be used to construct a personalized learning programme for specific groups of learners.

Box 2.2 NOCN Mission and Values statements

NOCN Mission

The Open College Network supports learning and widens opportunity by recognising achievement through credit-based courses and qualifications.

NOCN Values Statement

- A belief in the entitlement of people to gain recognition for their achievements in learning and to fulfil their potential.
- Respect for and encouragement of diversity in learners and learning approaches, partners and settings.
- A passion to make a difference to disadvantaged individuals, groups and communities.
- An ambition to open up opportunities for vocational progression and personal and social development.
- A commitment to integrity and ethical business practices.

(NOCN 2010)

Introducing the scheme of work

In this section we will be considering the importance of having a scheme of work and how to write one. First, let us look at what we mean by a 'scheme of work'.

What is a scheme of work?

Up to this point, we have tried to draw your attention to the wider notion of the curriculum and how this affects the way in which we deliver our programmes of learning. The scheme of work might be considered to be the document that is the manifestation of that curriculum. It is the mid- to long-term strategic plan in which you define your beliefs by aims and objectives and by the ways in which you intend to structure learning, teaching and assessment. Do we want our learners to develop as independent, autonomous learners, or are we content if they just do enough to complete an assignment or pass an exam? This would lead us to a discussion about 'deep and surface learning', but this is a topic for Chapter 4.

At this point you might like to turn back and refer to Table 2.1, the Morrison and Ridley model for analysis of the curriculum to remind yourself how your ideas about the purposes of education and your expectations of your learners will influence the way in which you approach and organize the learning experience.

Reflection 2.5

Referring to Table 2.1 and in the light of your reading so far, what are your preferred approaches to teaching, learning and assessment now?

Have they changed at all?

How would this affect the way in which you might design a scheme of work?

As the mid- to long-term plan for a programme of learning, the scheme of work sets out the way in which we intend to achieve the specific learning outcomes of the course in question as defined by those who design it, generally the awarding body, but it could be you, the teacher, in the case of an NOCN programme, for example.

Why do we need a scheme of work?

In the past, students on initial teacher training programmes often returned from their placements with tales of schemes of work that were written on the back of an envelope or their mentors would claim that they were 'in their head'. In these days of greater accountability to Senior Management and ultimately to OFSTED, this is less frequently, if ever the case. Many institutions have their own template for a scheme of work and also lesson plans in order to present a corporate policy towards the planning of learning: this in itself might be seen as a statement of the institution's 'hidden curriculum'. So, why is the scheme of work seen as such an important feature?

Reflection 2.6

The importance of this mid- to long-term planning might seem to be obvious. We hope it is, but it is worth spending a few moments considering this.

List all the reasons that you can think of justifying the need for a scheme of work.

We hope that you would come up with some of the following and maybe more:

- It is a way of organizing the content of a programme in a logical order to ensure learner development of knowledge, understanding and skills.
- It enables us to plan strategies that are appropriate to specific topics in a way that will enhance learning.
- It is a guide to lesson planning.
- It will enable us to plan when and how we will assess learning either through formative or summative procedures (we will discuss this in Chapter 5).
- It enables us to plan ahead for special resources that might need to be booked such as a computer suite, fitness testing equipment, visiting speakers or visits to external venues (Chapter 6 will deal with this).
- It will help your colleagues or line manager to integrate your scheme of work into the planning for the wider curriculum and enable somebody else to teach your lesson should you be absent.

- Tight planning of a scheme of work will, paradoxically, enable you to be more flexible, taking into account any unforeseen events or even adjusting to the needs of learners who advance more quickly than you had anticipated.

So, with all this in mind, we should ask the question, how should we go about designing a scheme of work and what should be in it?

Designing the scheme of work

What should be in the scheme of work?

Reflection 2.7

Thinking about the issues discussed above, make a list of what you think should be in a comprehensive scheme of work and justify your selection.

As we have said, many institutions will have their own templates and, generally, they will include the following (as should your answer to Reflection 2.7) and maybe more:

- *General information*: it is, first, worth making a note of the various factors that may affect our planning – how many weeks are there to complete the programme? How long is each session? And, if we are to plan programmes appropriate to learners' needs – how many students are there in the group? What is the group profile? What is their experience of the subject to date? Are there any students who might need special attention?
- *The aims, general objectives and learning outcomes*: these will be informed by the awarding body's specifications but will need to be organized in a logical order for our teaching purposes.
- *Content*: again this is where you will order the sequence of learning activities, probably informed by the aims, objectives and learning outcomes and taking into account activities such as assessments and planned visits.
- *Teaching and learning methods*: planning at this stage will ensure that you consider the most appropriate methods for each topic and plan for variety.
- *Assessment methods and timing*: this will, again, enable you to consider the most appropriate and valid methods for each topic or for the course overall (whether assignments, role play, presentations, exams or tests) and the timings. (Based on Petty 2004: 441–2)

Getting started

Given all this information, where then do we start with our design? One model that has been useful for a number of decades is Ralph Tyler's very simple model for curriculum design (1971). Figure 2.1 illustrates this: you will notice that the first

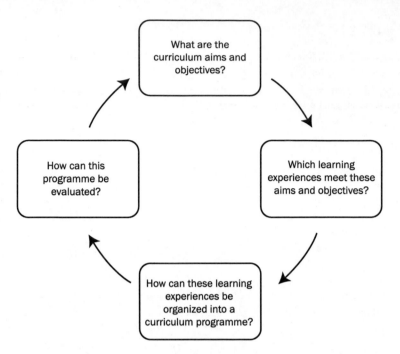

Figure 2.1 Tyler's model for curriculum design (1971)

premise is that the designer will need to know exactly what the aims, objectives and learning outcomes should be. In a way, this would suggest a 'Behaviourist', product approach to the curriculum and this has drawn much criticism, particularly from Progressive-Humanists who favour the process curriculum. However, as we have noted elsewhere, arguably, if the process of learning is a desired result of the learning programme, it might still be described as an 'outcome'.

Reflection 2.8

Using Tyler's model, sketch out a curriculum for one (or more) of the following:

- How to conduct an induction session for a gymnasium.
- How to research the fitness levels of members of a rugby team.
- How to organize a sports activity day for young people.

Using Tyler's model, we need to define what it is we would like our learners to achieve, our outcomes, since this gives us purpose and direction. Unless we are writing our own programme, as we might with NOCN, then generally the guidance we need might be found in the awarding bodies' specifications.

What does the scheme of work look like?

Reflection 2.9

Figure 2.2 is an example of the content of part of one unit from a BTEC National Diploma programme with the accompanying learning outcomes.

- If you were aiming to teach this module over a period of six three-hour sessions, what would be the best order to teach each topic?
- Why would you do it this way?

If you are unfamiliar with this topic, please choose another from any set of specifications.

Unit content

1 Understand the importance of lifestyle factors in the maintenance of health and wellbeing

Lifestyle factors: physical activity (recommendations and guidelines, health benefits, psychological benefits); alcohol (recommendations and guidelines, risks associated with excessive drinking, e.g. malnutrition, cancer, stroke, cirrhosis, hypertension, depression, mood swings); smoking (health risks, e.g. coronary heart disease, cancer, lung infections – bronchitis, emphysema); stress (health risks of excessive stress levels, e.g. hypertension, angina, stroke, heart attack, ulcers, depression, colitis); diet (benefits of a healthy diet, effects of poor nutrition, recommendations and guidelines, balance of good health)

2 Be able to assess the lifestyle of a selected individual

Lifestyle questionnaire: e.g. levels of physical activity, alcohol consumption, smoking, stress levels, diet, one-to-one consultation

Consultation: communication, e.g. questioning, listening skills, non-verbal communication, client confidentiality

3 Be able to provide advice on lifestyle improvement

Strategies: physical activity (ways to increase physical activity levels, e.g. walking, stair climbing, cycling); alcohol, e.g. seek alternatives, counselling and therapy, detoxification, self-help groups, alternative treatment and therapies; smoking, e.g. acupuncture, NHS smoking helpline, NHS stop-smoking services, nicotine replacement therapy; stress management techniques, e.g. assertiveness, goal setting, time management, physical activity, positive self-talk, relaxation, breathing; diet, e.g. timing of food intake, eating more or less of certain foods, food preparation; behaviour change, e.g. stages of change, common barriers, cognitive and behavioural strategies

4 Be able to plan a health-related physical activity programme for a selected individual

Collect information: e.g. personal goals, lifestyle, medical history, physical activity history, attitudes, motivation

Goal setting: goals (short-, medium- and long-term); targets (specific, measurable, achievable, realistic, time bound – SMART)

Principles of training: overload; specificity; progression; individual differences; variation; reversibility; frequency, intensity, time and type (FITT) principles

Appropriate activities: e.g. walking, cycling, hiking, swimming

Exercise intensity: e.g. rating of perceived exertion (RPE), maximum heart rate, maximum heart rate reserve

---

Figure 2.2 Module from BTEC National in Sport and Exercise Sciences
Source: BN018434 – Specification – Edexcel Level 3 BTEC Nationals in Sport and Exercise Sciences – Issue 1 – October 2006 © Edexcel Limited 2006

If you were planning a series of lessons as in Reflection 2.9 how would you draw up your plan? As we have said, you would possibly have to work from a template provided by the institution, but you should really be able to make your own decisions about the format and ensure that you do take into consideration all the factors we have mentioned so far. Figure 2.3, opposite, is a part of a scheme of work using such a template. Consider the issues raised in Reflection 2.10 and try to devise your own scheme of work for the unit in Figure 2.2.

Reflection 2.10

Figure 2.3 is an example of the first three weeks of a scheme of work designed for a programme at a college of Further Education:

- Are the aims and learning outcomes clear?
- What do we know about the learners in this group?
- How might we adapt our teaching and learning activities to accommodate their learning preferences? Is there sufficient variety in the activities?
- Given that we only have three weeks of this topic shown here, is the sequence of learning appropriate?
- Have the resources been well planned in advance?
- How will the teacher ensure that learning has taken place?

Reflection 2.10 and the section, 'What should be in a scheme of work' should enable you to develop your own ideas about the design of this important document. But, above all, it will be a reflection not only of what you need to teach as defined by the programme specifications, but also of your own principles about what kinds of people you would like your learners to develop into. This will become clear through the kinds of activities that you plan for them, the way that you approach their learning and even the kinds of resources that you use to support their learning.

The scheme of work, then, is a declaration of your intent.

Summary

In this chapter we have focused on the wider implications of curriculum design and the various factors that influence it. We hope that it will have given you greater insight into the ideologies that drive it and the models that derive from them and how they are mirrored in the courses and programmes that we teach. It is important to understand the difference between the product curriculum and the process curriculum because these ideas will affect the way in which we organize the learning experiences for our students. This is the subject of the next two chapters.

If, at the end of the programme, the curriculum is to lead to more than a certificate which merely proves that certain knowledge or competence has been acquired (the product), but rather it also leads to the development of the student as an independent learner with the personal skills to enter the world of employment and/or higher education (the process), then we need to plan those learning experiences very carefully and very thoroughly.

Subject/Unit/Module	Instructing Physical Activity and Exercise		Subject Lecturer	
Programme Name and Course Code	BTEC National Diploma Sport and Exercise Science	**Group**	4NDSX-0809-G	**Hours per week**	2
Academic Year	2009/2010	**No of Weeks**	34	**Start and Completion Date of Scheme of Work**	14/09/09–25/06/10

Learning Styles of the Group (Note the number of students with each learning styles of the group)	Group Profile (Note student mix, those requiring support, etc)	Health and Safety (Note any issues you may have for this subject)
Pragmatist 2 Reflector 1 Activist 15 Theorist 2 Visual 11 Auditory 1 Kinesthetic 8	The group consists of 20 students. The group has very similar ability levels in both theoretical and practical elements of the course. There are no additional support mechanisms in place and all students have completed a BSA and appropriate support given. Group dynamics: Male students 12 Female students 8	• Keep fire exits clear at all times • Know the location of fire alarms, fire extinguishers and fire exits. • Keep aisles between desks clear of bags, kit, etc. • Put equipment away after session • Must wear correct clothing for practical activity

Week No	Topic area/Indicative Content Include opportunities for contextualized advice and guidance	Assessment Note all checks on learning to take place e.g. Q/A, quiz, observation	Resources Include technicians/LSA support present/guest speakers, e-learning and differentiated learning materials	Basic/Key Skills; Study Support	Every Child Matters Ref/Comments
1 w/c 21/09/09	**Introduction to course unit.** **Principles of safe and effective exercise.** **Components of Fitness.** **Adaptations to Training.** **Principles of Training.** **Set Assignment 1.** Why do people exercise? Introductory student	Feedback, Q&A, Discussion, Tutor observation, Worksheets, Set tasks, Completion of Assignment 1.	Myself, Students, Course specification, Whiteboard and pen, Handouts, Worksheets, PowerPoint Presentation.	C2.1a C2.2 N2.1 N2.2 ICT2.1 ICT2.2 ICT2.3	1.2 1.3 1.2.6 2.1 2.2 3.4 3.7

(Continued)

Week No	Topic area/Indicative Content Include opportunities for contextualized advice and guidance	Assessment Note all checks on learning to take place e.g. Q/A, quiz, observation	Resources Include technicians/LSA support present/guest speakers, e-learning and differentiated learning materials	Basic/Key Skills; Study Support	Every Child Matters Ref/Comments
	tasks to list as many reasons of why people take part in exercise. Recap over the five components of fitness. Definition of each. Examples from students and explanations of each. Link to fitness plans. Introduction to adaptations to training. Adaptations to aerobic endurance training. Lungs, heart, blood and blood vessels, muscles and bones. Introduction to the principles of training and how they link to programme design.				4.3 4.6 5.2 5.3
2 w/c 05/10/09	**Health and safety for exercise sessions.** Introduction to health and safety for exercise sessions. The Health and Safety at Work Act. Link this to the training of our participant. PARQ – examples shown and explanations of why they are used. The Exercise and Fitness Code of Ethics. Cover the 4 principles. Explain. Introduction to Contraindications. Examples of contraindications to exercise.	Feedback, Q&A, Discussion, Tutor observation, Worksheets, Set tasks, Completion of Assignment 1.	Myself, Students, Whiteboard and pen, PARQ's, Handouts, Worksheets, PowerPoint Presentation.	C2.1a C2.2 N2.1 N2.2 ICT2.1 ICT2.2 ICT2.3	1.2 1.3 1.2.6 2.1 2.2 3.4 3.7 4.3 4.6
3 w/c 12/10/09	**Health and safety for exercise sessions.** Benefits, purpose and objectives of a warm up. Components of a warm up. – Pulse raiser, joint mobility and dynamic stretching. Explanation, benefits and examples given of each. Components of a cool-down – lowering the heart rate, maintenance stretching and developmental stretching. Explanation, benefits and examples.	Feedback, Q&A, Discussion, Tutor observation, Worksheets, Set tasks, Completion of Assignment 1.	Myself, Students, Whiteboard and pen, Handouts, Worksheets, Interactive whiteboard, PowerPoint Presentation.	C2.1a C2.2 N2.1 N2.2 ICT2.1 ICT2.2 ICT2.3	1.2 1.3 1.2.6 2.1 2.2 3.4 3.7

Figure 2.3 Exemplar scheme of work

The Key Skills agenda (Chapter 3) addresses exactly these issues and seeks to seamlessly 'embed' the skills into the curriculum, which is another aspect of curriculum design that we have not really touched upon here. But the planning is only the first stage, what is most important is the face-to-face contact between teacher and learner, and this is the subject of Chapter 4 which addresses the teaching and learning experience. It is here that Stenhouse's 'reality of the curriculum' is truly experienced.

3

Embedding Key Skills and Functional Skills in the Sport and Leisure curriculum

In this chapter we will be looking at:

- The development of the Key Skills and Functional Skills curricula
- The main Key Skills and Functional Skills and their component parts
- Designing learning programmes that embed Key and Functional Skills
- Developing ways of supporting learners in the development of their skills
- Barriers to learning key and functional skills
- Embedding Personal Learning and Thinking Skills (PLTS)

Introduction

Along with a concern for a perceived disaffection for schooling, as identified in the first chapter, there has been a further consistent belief that many learners have been leaving the compulsory education system ill-equipped to take a full and meaningful, independent role in society. They have been ill-equipped particularly in the skills of literacy and numeracy, but also in the more general life-skills that would make them more attractive to employers.

These concerns were reflected in the Moser Report (DfEE 1999) which 'concluded that one in five adults had literacy skills below those expected of an eleven year old' (Appleyard and Appleyard 2009: 1).

Given the implications of these alarming statistics, it is no longer acceptable for the practising teacher of Sport and Leisure (or teachers of any subject for that matter), to pay attention only to the content of learners' work and to ignore accuracy in use of language or of numeracy. Furthermore, in this technological age of electronic communications, it is essential that learners develop skills in ICT that enhance their ability to use such skills effectively in the wider social context beyond computer gaming and the text message.

Reflection 3.1

Box 3.1 is an example of an assignment written by a student following a BTEC National programme in Sport and Exercise Science. The content seems to be acceptable, but how would you mark this in terms of the student's engagement with literacy skills? What specific problems can you identify?

While many subject teachers may lack confidence in delivering and assessing key skills or functional skills, it is now expected that they should all be able to recognize opportunities within the subject for development and assessment of these skills and, indeed, should work towards their own development in them. This is reflected in the requirements for trainee teachers on any training programme to achieve the TDA standards or the Minimum Core in the skills. Of course, it is also expected that institutions (schools, colleges and Adult Education Centres) should provide expert

---

Box 3.1 Case study of a student assessment

The context is a L3 National Sport and Exercise Sciences learner

Criterion: P6 Describe three data collection techniques in quantitative research in the sport and exercise sciences.

One common method for collection of this data involves an observer making hand-written notes, comments, and sketches. This often proves to be inefficient in field-based evaluation environments.

This is more digitally used as in recorders can be used to any sort of computering tool which records to catch any information needed.

Most interviews are can be good because when sitting face to face you can see all the behaviour change from the person being interviewed and this could be easier for the examiner to see when lies or attitude change is being taken place, but on the other hand this could also be a bad way because if the interviewee is calm and keeping a moderate face talking there way out of questions or at most times not choosing to reply to comments then the interviewer wouldn't be getting much information.

If I was to set up a interview myself I would study the person I'm interviewing to back up any questions that the interviewee may have a good answer towards, talking about mainly police interviews, I would firstly set closed questions so that the inter-viewee has a structured answer and then as time goes on I would freely start speak-ing and let the interview flow within asking my own questions towards what kind of answers are giving by the person.

advice from specialists to support subject teachers and lecturers. We shall see how this is managed when we analyse models of embedding.

So what is the proposed solution to these shortcomings?

This chapter will examine the background and the development of the Key Skills and, more recently, the Functional Skills agenda, and will analyse the content of their curricula to enable the Sport and Leisure Teacher to support their learners more effectively.

The background to and rise of Key Skills

In the 1980s, programmes written by the original Business Education Council (BEC) and the Technical Education Council (TEC), which later combined as the now more well-known BTEC, included an assessment of what they termed as 'common skills'. These included numeracy and literacy, and later, with the development of electronic technology, ICT.

Interestingly, BTEC policy (reflecting their learner-centred philosophy as discussed in Chapter 2) proposed that, wherever possible, these common skills should be integrated into the subject curriculum, thus ensuring that they were contextualized and made more meaningful to the learner.

This is all the more significant since BTEC pre-empted current policy which is to do precisely that – to integrate 'functional' skills wherever possible into the subject curriculum. Clearly BTEC was very conscious of the need to motivate learners by ensuring that the skills were learnt and assessed in meaningful contexts.

In the 1990s, the General National Vocational Qualification (GNVQ) was introduced. Like the BTEC programmes, this was not a qualification to actually qualify the learner to work in an industry, but was intended to be a preparation for working in specific occupations and towards eventually gaining such qualifications. Designed very much on the BTEC model, GNVQs required learners to achieve what now became known as 'Key' Skills, again including literacy, numeracy and ICT. They also developed a range of personal skills, which became known as the 'Wider' Key Skills (Working with Others, Improving Own Learning and Performance, and Problem Solving), and were intended to develop skills that were seen as essential to personal, social and vocational development. The underpinning principle of the Key Skills agenda is that the skills should be transferable to any aspect of life and that they should be seen in the context of a coherent plan for learner development (Donovan 2005: 117).

Similar and parallel to the Key Skills agenda is the Adult Literacy and Numeracy programme (ALAN) which mirrors its standards and is assessed entirely by portfolio, thus ensuring that the opportunity to relate the use of the skills to real situations is possible.

Reflection 3.2

For each of the Key/Functional Skills (Literacy/English; Numeracy/Maths; ICT) think of at least three contexts where knowledge of and competency in them are an essential asset to following a career in Sport and Leisure.

Following the Dearing Report (1996), Curriculum 2000 proposed a curriculum that was intended to promote equity between the range of qualifications, whether considered academic (A levels and GCSEs) or vocational (NVQs, GNVQs, National Diplomas), and 'Key Skills' at levels 1–4 were available to all as 'stand-alone' qualifications, incidentally, attracting UCAS points. In fact, Key Skills became available from level 1 to level 4 to learners across the education and training spectrum including undergraduates and NVQ trainees.

Since the demise of Curriculum 2000 and the publication of the Tomlinson Report (2004) that proposed an integrated curriculum of Diplomas (Chapters 1 and 2), the notion of 'Functional Skills' has been floated and, at the time of writing, they are set to replace 'Key Skills'.

The idea is that the essential skills should be specifically related to the learner's social and occupational environment, thus ensuring that they are seen to be relevant to their needs. Key skills were previously highly criticized for often being irrelevant and merely a repetition of GCSE Maths and English by another name. For example, what on earth would be the relevance of knowing how to calculate the volume of a cylinder to a student of Sport and Leisure unless it be to check the accuracy of the contents of an energy drinks can?

So now, although the skills are assessed by a generic test, the content of the Functional Skills curriculum is intended to directly reflect the proposed working environment of the learner. Therefore, it should be possible to 'embed' this curriculum fully into the occupational subject curriculum. The notion of 'embedding' and the impact this has on the planning of the Sport and Leisure curriculum and lessons are the subject of one of the following sections.

Reflection 3.3

Consider each of the Functional/Key Skills:

- Literacy/English
- Numeracy/Maths
- ICT

Try to think of activities taken from a Sport and Leisure programme on which you teach at any level, which might provide an opportunity to assess any aspect of each one.

Although it may be noticed that the 'wider' Key Skills appear to be missing here, the attributes that they were intended to develop are now subsumed into a programme of Personal, Learning and Thinking Skills, affectionately known as PeLTS. Again, we shall visit these later.

What are the Key Skills?

As we have seen, Key Skills are skills that are transferable from one context to another, enabling learners to develop personal effectiveness for adult and working life. As Edexcel Specifications for National Diplomas note:

Learners need the chance to show current and future employers that they can:

- communicate effectively
- use number
- use ICT
- work well with others
- manage their own development
- solve problems

(Edexcel 2007: 231)

We shall consider these in the context of the Sport and Leisure Industry and, of course, what this means for the development of the Sport and Leisure curriculum. Obviously, the skills will be developmental through each stage and we will consider each of the first three in some depth and the 'softer' skills more generally.

The following information may be found on the QCDA website (www.qcda. gov.uk) which also gives more detail of the precise skills under each category, such as 'Interpret information: Read and understand tables, charts, graphs and diagrams' (Application of number level 1).

Communication

The skills are developmental, for example, leading from simple one-to-one discussion to taking part in a group discussion, to demonstrating skill in oral communication, depending on the level. Students also have to read, comprehend and synthesize information, and write different types of documents. Communication is perhaps the easiest of the Skills to develop opportunities for learners to demonstrate their competence. An assignment that requires the learner to read literature on diet or keeping fit, for example, and to present a short talk on their findings would provide such opportunities for each of these aspects of communication (Table 3.1, opposite).

Application of Number

The skills in the use of number that the learner must demonstrate at the different levels include interpreting information from different sources, such as tables and charts; carrying out calculations to do with amounts, sizes, scales or proportion; handling statistics and using formulae; and interpreting the results of their calculations (Table 3.2, opposite).

As we have already suggested, although it may be more difficult to find opportunities to develop such skills through the Sport and Leisure curriculum, they do exist at all levels. For example, at basic levels, a learner might be asked to estimate and measure out how many mini-soccer pitches could be marked out in a given area for a small tournament; or how much the organizers should charge per team in order to cover the costs of the hire of a hall. On the other hand, at higher levels, much more sophisticated calculations would be required to perhaps assess fitness levels from an athlete's

Table 3.1 Technical descriptors for Key Skills Communication showing progression between levels

Level 1	Level 2	Level 3
Take part in one-to-one discussion or a group discussion	Take part in a group discussion	Take part in a group discussion
	Give a short talk	Make a formal presentation using an image or other support material
Read and obtain information	Read and summarize information	Read and synthesize information
Write two different types of documents	Write two different types of documents each one giving different information	Write two different types of documents, each one giving different information about complex subjects

Table 3.2 Technical descriptors for Key Skills Application of Number showing progression between levels

Level 1	Level 2	Level 3
Interpret information from two different sources	Interpret information from a suitable source	Plan an activity and get relevant information from relevant sources
Carry out and check calculations to do with amounts or sizes; scales or proportion; handling statistics	Use your information to carry out calculations to do with amounts or sizes; scales or proportion; handling statistics; using formulae	Use this information to carry out multi-stage calculations to do with amounts or sizes; scales or proportion; handling statistics; using formulae
Interpret the results of your calculations and present findings	Interpret the results of your calculations and present findings	Interpret the results of your calculations and present findings and justify your methods

physical data or to analyse usage of a leisure centre from membership or attendance data.

Information and communication technology (ICT)

Here the learner is required to use electronic sources to search for information for specific purposes, at higher levels using different sources and criteria. They then have to enter and develop the information before presenting it accurately and, at higher levels, combining text, images and number (Table 3.3).

Table 3.3 Technical descriptors for Key Skills Information and Communication Technology showing progression between levels

Level 1	Level 2	Level 3
Find and select relevant information	Search for and select information to meet your needs	Search for information using different sources, and multiple search criteria
Enter and develop information to suit the task	Enter and develop information to suit the task and derive new information	Enter and develop the information and derive new information
Develop the presentation so that the final output is accurate and fit for purpose	Present combined information such as text with image, text with number, image with number	Present combined information such as text with image, text with number, image with number

Many (though not necessarily all) young people today are familiar with modern electronic technology, although this may be largely practised in a recreational context. So the teacher's task here is to apply the standards to realistic situations that will enable their learners to develop their skills to efficiently seek out information from the vast store now available and apply them to enhance effective communication in a working environment. Again, it would not be so difficult to design opportunities for learners to demonstrate their skill in ICT through researching information from internet sources, for example, and then presenting their findings either in an assignment or perhaps a PowerPoint presentation.

However, it should also be remembered that, equally, many adults may be unfamiliar with, and even fearful of, technology and may need much sympathetic guidance. This we shall discuss later under 'Supporting Learner Development'.

Reflection 3.4

Consider the scheme of work in Figure 2.3 (Chapter 2). Using the charts in Tables 3.1, 3.2 and 3.3, try to identify activities that will help to generate evidence for any of the skills listed, or devise some of your own.

The Wider Key Skills

Although the key skills of Communication, Numeracy and ICT are assessed by both portfolio and external test, the Wider Skills are assessed by portfolio alone which means that opportunities to provide evidence of their achievement can be generated during the normal course of studies. These are skills that might be described as 'process' skills since they reflect the attributes that the learner needs to develop in order to become a better learner and more effective member of society. Improving own Learning would suggest that they could learn to become more independent and take responsibility for their own learning. Solving Problems is a skill that will, again, help develop autonomy, and Working with Others suggests that they will learn to contribute to the good of the whole and respect the contributions of others (Table 3.4).

Table 3.4 Summarizing the Wider Skills

Criterion	Working with Others	Improving Own Learning	Problem Solving
1	Understand the implications of working with others	Setting targets and devising an action plan	How to identify and solve problems
2	Identify and carry out tasks within a team	Develop strategies to improve own learning	Develop a plan to solve a problem
3	Evaluate the work of the team	Review progress and modify the action plan	Evaluate how successful the plan has been in solving the problem

Reflection 3.5

With reference to the Wider Key Skills listed in Table 3.4 and the scheme of work in Chapter 2 (Figure 2.3), do the same exercise as in Reflection 3.4 and try to identify or create opportunities for learners to generate evidence for the Wider Skills.

Adult Literacy, Adult Numeracy and ICT Skills

A number of our adult learners will possibly be working towards achievement under the Adult Literacy and Adult Numeracy (ALAN) programme. Launched in 2001 as part of the government's Skills for Life Public Service agreement and in response to concern over the low levels of adult literacy and numeracy, targets were set to improve the basic skills of the 2.25 million adults by 2010. The standards, set by QCDA, 'Are very closely linked to the key skills qualifications standards . . . [and] are technical documents intended for use by those working in education and training to form the basis of curricula, qualifications and assessment material' (QCDA 2009).

Similar to Key Skills assessments, they are assessed by externally examined tests covering knowledge and understanding, but learners also have to produce a portfolio of evidence showing practical application of the skills. Some of the work carried out under your Sport and Leisure programmes may well form part of their portfolios of evidence, and this is something to bear in mind when planning for learning and assessment.

Reflection 3.6

As we have noted, many adults might be fearful of using ICT.

How might you help them to overcome this fear and develop their skills in a way that will enhance their capacity to learn?

What are the Functional Skills?

At the time of writing, the Functional Skills project is still at the pilot stage of development. However, they will be launched for general delivery and assessment in 2010. Although the Leitch Report (DfEE 2006) focused on addressing what was perceived as a deficit in vocational skills, undoubtedly there was an implication that without an improvement in national standards in English, Mathematics and ICT to support it, there would be little commensurate improvement overall. The challenge to 'close the skills gap' by 2020 would fail at the first hurdle, so the government have made the development of the Functional Skills agenda a national priority. At the same time, this development is seen to support the Every Child Matters agenda by ensuring that all learners have the opportunity to 'gain the most out of life, learning and work'. According to QCA (2007):

> Functional skills in English, mathematics and information and communication technology (ICT) help people to gain the most out of life, learning and work.
>   The skills are learning tools that enable people:
>
> - to apply their knowledge and understanding to everyday life
> - to engage competently and confidently with others
> - to solve problems in both familiar and unfamiliar situations
> - to develop personally and professionally as positive citizens who can actively contribute to society.

Functional Skills thus relate to the development of skills in English, Mathematics and ICT. Note the change in descriptors from 'Communication' and 'Numeracy'. However, the rhetoric and principles remain the same as for Key Skills: 'The term "functional" should be considered in the broad sense of providing learners with the skills and abilities they need to take an active and responsible role in their communities, everyday life, the workplace and educational settings' (QCA 2007: 7, 19 and 27).
    The specifications for each skills area are far more detailed than those for Key Skills and, although it is expected that Functional Skills should be delivered in the context of the general subject (in our case, of course, Sport and Leisure), they are assessed entirely by specific tests, some external and some internal.

English

According to QCA (2007: 7): 'Functional English requires learners to communicate in ways that make them effective and involved citizens, to operate confidently and to convey their ideas and opinions clearly.'

Mathematics

According to QCA (2007: 19): 'Functional Mathematics requires learners to use mathematics in ways that make them effective and involved as citizens, to operate confidently in life, and to work in a wide range of contexts.'

ICT

According to QCA (2007: 27): 'Functional ICT requires learners to use technology in ways that make them effective and involved as citizens, to operate confidently in life, and to work in a wide range of contexts.'

Embedding Key and Functional Skills into the Occupational Subject Curriculum

The notion of embedding key skills and functional skills into the learning and teaching programme is not a new idea. Indeed, although they may not have used the current buzz word, the principle of assessing Common Skills through subject assignment work could be found in the BTEC Diplomas of the 1980s and 1990s. As we have seen, Key Skills are now assessed not only through completion of a test but also by presentation of a portfolio in which evidence of practical application of the skills is identified. Embedding Key Skills means, therefore, creating or recognizing opportunities for learners to apply those skills to any other aspect of their learning programme. This might be planned by the teacher when writing the scheme of work or lesson plan, or even presented as a task for the learner to review their own work to recognize where they might identify evidence of achievement for themselves.

Essentially, then, embedding the skills is intended to create opportunities for learners to use them in realistic contexts that will make them more meaningful and thus motivate learners to develop their skills still further.

Although Functional Skills are examined purely through a series of tests, learning should be facilitated by embedding them in the same way into the subject programme. The tests themselves are set in realistic working environments. Figures 3.1 and 3.2, on the following pages, are examples of tests related to the Sport and Leisure curriculum. For more information, see www.ocr.org.uk/qualifications/index.html.

Supporting learner development of Key and Functional Skills

Common problems, disabilities and learning difficulties in the Key Skills

As a teacher of Sport and Leisure, you will undoubtedly encounter a number of learners who experience difficulties with any or all of the Key Skills to varying degrees. As we noted in the introduction, these difficulties cannot simply be ignored in favour of content of the subject. Indeed, they may even inhibit our learners' enjoyment and ability to understand it. So we have a responsibility to them to be aware of any problems they may have with any of the skills and to support them in order to maximize their learning. The Key Skills and Functional Skills curricula exist as a guide to our expectations of the standards they should achieve.

It is important to acknowledge that these problems are not confined to those learners with identified disabilities and learning difficulties, and that most of our learners will need some help to improve one or two aspects of their Key Skills. This may be a problem with the use of the apostrophe or in giving a verbal presentation; or with converting currencies, or with saving and editing documents. A good starting

Scenario

You are a member of Meadowbrook Sports Club. Having read the Chairman's letter (Document 1) and the comments on the e-noticeboard (Document 2), you decide to email all members of the Club persuading them of the need to act and save the Club.

TASK 1 – Reading (19 marks)

In preparation for writing the email, use information from Documents 1 and 2 to answer the following questions.

You do not need to write in sentences.

1.   What is the purpose of each document?

(2 marks)

2.   Explain what is meant by the term 'specialist facilities' as used in the documents. Identify one example of a specialist facility which may have to close.

(2 marks)

3.   According to Joan, her son will be seriously affected if he has to travel further to train. Identify three specific effects this would have on him.

(3 marks)

4.   Compare the views of Dipak and Saul in Document 2 about the subscriptions paid at the Club.

(4 marks)

5.   Compare the views of the Chairman in Document 1 with those of Tom in Document 2.

(4 marks)

6.   Describe how each document has been written to convey meaning effectively. You should consider:

*   use of language
*   style
*   structure.

(4 marks)

TASK 2 – Writing (19 marks)

Write a formal email to all members of the Club persuading them of the need to act and save the Club.

In your email, you should:

*   explain why you feel the need to write to them

*   give your views on what the Club and members should do.

Remember to write in sentences, using accurate spelling, punctuation and grammar.

Figure 3.1 Exemplar test for Functional Skills English produced by OCR for the pilot

DOCUMENT 1

MEADOWBROOK SPORTS CLUB
124 Field Lane
Coran
Cheshire
CN11 2AQ
Clubhouse: 01234 567689

4 January 2009

Dear Member

As you may be aware from our last meeting, Meadowbrook Sports Club is facing an uncertain future.

We are short of funds, as the only money we have comes from our members' subscriptions and a small contribution from the Parish Council. We cannot, therefore, continue with our present low level of subscriptions and maintain the breadth of sporting excellence the club is renowned for. It is also important to appreciate that member numbers, particularly amongst the under-18 age group, have been falling for some time. This has been made worse over the past 2 years as more leisure gyms and keep-fit clubs have opened in the area, which have carried out extensive marketing and membership campaigns.

The Committee is considering a variety of ways forward for the Club, including closure of some of our more specialist facilities such as gymnastics and climbing, which require expensive equipment and expert coaches. Although we would hope to avoid it, complete closure may have to be considered if the situation does not improve.

We have carried out a survey of Club members, via the members' e-noticeboard, but we are disappointed by the poor response and negativity. The Committee feels that many members have not grasped the severity of the situation; continuing with the current level of subscription while maintaining our current facilities is not a feasible option.

We will continue to monitor the situation and options closely and will be discussing this with all of you at the Annual General Meeting next month. In the meantime, we would hope that members will continue to give their full support to the Club and the promotion of the sporting ideals we have always stood for.

Yours faithfully

Nik Walker

Nik Walker
Chairman

Figure 3.1 Exemplar test for Functional Skills English produced by OCR for the pilot (*Continued*)

DOCUMENT 2

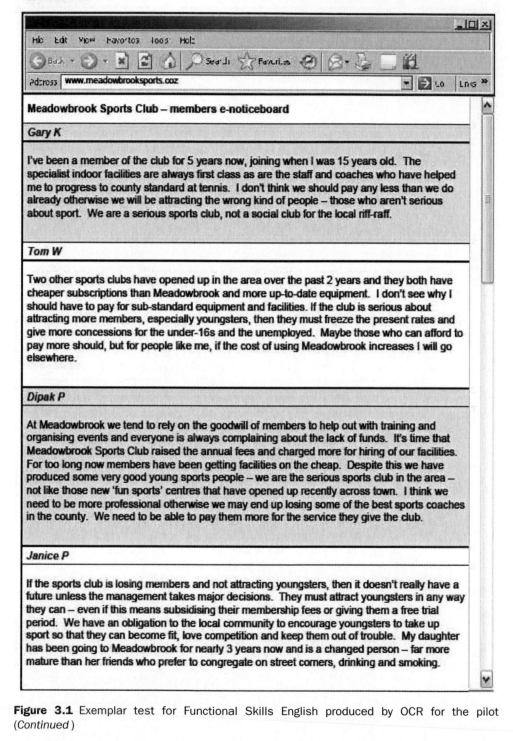

Figure 3.1 Exemplar test for Functional Skills English produced by OCR for the pilot (*Continued*)

point would be diagnostic assessments that identify individual strengths and areas for further development so that we can plan sessions that present opportunities to develop learners' skills or modify our own teaching to make it more accessible for them.

As teachers we need to ensure that our own skills and our understanding of language, number and ICT are sufficiently honed to be able to identify where there are problems and to be able to deal with them (Appleyard and Appleyard 2009: 7). Perhaps the first activity should be to try out a diagnostic assessment task for ourselves!

You might wish to revisit Reflection 3.1 completed earlier in the chapter as a check on your own familiarity with the Key Skills.

Reflection 3.7

Can you identify any specific problems for the learner in Box 3.1?

How could you help them to address their problems?

Who might you consult if you felt that this was beyond your own expertise?

Of course, each of the Key Skills subjects brings its own specific problems, but there are also some that are generic that may be generated by common 'barriers to learning'.

Weight To Lose (WTL) is advertised as a new diet tablet to help people lose weight.

A TV programme wants to test whether this claim is true or not.

To test this, 47 male members of a health club are selected and divided Into 4 groups, A, B, C and D.

They are weighed before and after the experiment. The results are shown in the Experiment Results tables.

The groups have different exercise programmes and diets:

• Regular walking, calorie-controlled diet and placebo tablets. (Group A)

• Regular walking, calorie-controlled diet and WTL tablets. (Group B)

• Working-out five times a week, calorie-controlled diet and placebo tablets. (Group C)

• Working-out five times a week, calorie-controlled diet and WTL tablets. (Group D)

Note: A placebo tablet is a fake tablet that has no active ingredients. However, the men taking the fake tablet will not know it is fake and so they might believe it is a diet tablet.

Figure 3.2 Exemplar Functional Skills Maths Paper produced by OCR for the pilot

Experiment Results

Regular walking, calorie-controlled diet and placebo tablets. (Group A)

Member	Age (years)	Weight change (kg)
1	31	−1
2	25	−9
3	29	−5.5
4	24	−7.5
5	30	−2.5
6	32	+3
7	23	−1.5
8	28	−11.5
9	27	+4
10	31	+2
11	26	−0.5

Regular walking, calorie-controlled diet and WTL tablets. (Group B)

Member	Age (years)	Weight change (kg)
12	23	−2
13	28	+2
14	31	−6.5
15	24	−5
16	25	−6.5
17	30	+0.5
18	24	−9
19	30	−5
20	31	−3.5
21	27	+2.5
22	27	−5.5
23	29	−1.5
24	29	+2.5

Working-out five times a week, calorie-controlled diet and placebo tablets. (Group C)

Member	Age (years)	Weight change (kg)
25	28	−2.5
26	18	−1
27	30	−10
28	27	−8.5
29	23	−4.5
30	28	−3
31	23	−3
32	27	−4
33	25	−7.5
34	31	−6.5
35	27	−9.5

Working-out five times a week, calorie-controlled diet and WTL tablets (Group D)

Member	Age (years)	Weight change (kg)
36	28	−10
37	29	−11.5
38	32	0
39	30	−2.5
40	31	−11
41	25	−8.5
42	25	−0.5
43	28	−2.5
44	31	−0.5
45	25	−10.5
46	27	−1.5
47	30	0

Figure 3.2 Exemplar Functional Skills Maths Paper produced by OCR for the pilot (*Continued*)
Source: OCR Functional Skills Mathematics Level 2/Task and Answer Booklet/March 2008

Generic barriers to learning Key Skills

Armitage et al. (2007) identify three main categories of barriers to learning: we would do well to briefly examine these in relation to the problems that learners may have with Key Skills. They are: *educational*, which implies that the learner has either specific difficulties or low motivation to learn; *institutional*, where the school or college may have not given sufficient support to the learner; and *societal*, which places the problems in the context of the learner's role in and relationship with society as a whole.

Reflection 3.8

What do you think are the barriers that the learners in Box 3.2 might face? How might their teachers help them to overcome the barriers?

Box 3.2 Case studies of barriers to learning

Consider the following case studies: what 'barriers' to effective learning might they encounter?

Clive is a 17-year-old who left school a year ago with three very low grade GCSEs. Although he was disruptive at school, he is a fanatical footballer, has played in the local professional club's youth squad and is bitterly disappointed that he was not selected for their Football Academy. He plays every Sunday and trains two or three times a week, but will find any opportunity to play. Realizing that he will need to get qualifications for work, he has reluctantly been persuaded to enrol at the local college on a BTEC First Diploma in Sport.

Kathy is a 30-year-old mother of two who left school at 16. Although she worked for a few years as a shop assistant, she has spent most of her married life looking after the family. In her mid-twenties she developed an interest in keep-fit and now has enrolled on an aerobics teachers' course intending to make a new career. Her husband has just been made redundant and is looking for a new career too.

Chris is 18 and left school with a BTEC National in Sport Science. Determined to build a career in sport, although he's not sure exactly what kind of job, he is about to start a Sport Science degree at university. His parents are unable to give him much financial support.

The point that Armitage et al. make here is that, although these barriers might well be considered as separate causes of a learner's barriers to their competence in the Key Skills, they are most probably interlinked. Problems with sentence structure, for example, might have arisen from a lack of opportunities to read quality literature at home or from a poor relationship with a teacher at school, or both. The former could be considered societal while the latter could be educational and/or institutional. But it is helpful to consider these categories when we try to understand the issues facing particular learners if we are to be able to help them. Indeed, in the context of the Every Child Matters policy, it is essential.

Some specific disabilities and learning difficulties

There is insufficient space in this publication to consider these in depth, and in any case that is really the task of more specialist books such as the Minimum Core Series by Learning Matters (2009), already referred to above. Clearly, if teachers do encounter identified, or even suspected, problems as severe as this they should seek the advice of specialist support teachers. Nevertheless, as we have previously noted, learners with such problems will be members of our classes and we should be prepared to adapt our teaching accordingly.

The list of specific difficulties includes:

- deaf or partially hearing learners;
- blind or partially sighted learners;
- learners with mental health problems;
- learners with dyslexia;
- learners with physical disabilities;
- learners with learning difficulties;
- learners with autistic spectrum disorder.

The ability of learners in each category to engage with the Key Skills and Functional Skills may be challenged to varying degrees of severity and, of course, since we are concerned with the whole of the Lifelong Learning sector, we should perhaps also bear in mind that ageing may exacerbate some of those problems, relating, for example, to hearing and sight. However, there are strategies that can be adopted to alleviate the problems that these learners encounter, or at least to try to ensure that they do not find the learning challenging purely because of their disability. To this extent, and in the spirit of Every Child (Learner) Matters, we should ensure that the learning is personalized for them, in particular.

Clearly, first, we might hope that there would be a learning assistant available and you should discuss your lesson and the possible strategies that would be most appropriate with them well before the lesson. But you too can plan to accommodate such learners:

- Make sure that you speak clearly and, if necessary, be aware that some may need to lip-read.
- Give clear information and instructions.
- Repeat yourself and provide visual stimuli (handouts or PowerPoint).
- Break down tasks into manageable components.

- Use coloured paper for handouts particularly an issue for dyslexia sufferers.
- Customize ICT systems using the Accessibility options.
- Adapt keyboards.
- Use voice input software.
- Ensure that the learners have a safe environment in which to work. This is particularly important for those with Autistic Spectrum Disorders (ASD).

Source: Appleyard and Appleyard (2009); Clarke (2006); Peart (2009)

Reflection 3.9

Consider the scheme of work in Chapter 2 (Figure 2.3).

What adaptations might you need to make for learners with dyscalculia, dyslexia or ADS in your lessons?

Personal Learning and Thinking Skills (PLTS)

Earlier in this chapter we mentioned the 'Wider Key Skills' which became a part of the GNVQ and National Diploma curriculum. Interestingly, these seem to have been revived under the title of Personal Learning and Thinking Skills (PLTS – affectionately known as PeLTS) associated with the new 14–19 Diplomas discussed in Chapter 2. It is worthy of note that employers, represented by the Sector Skills Councils, played a major role in developing the Diplomas and specifically in identifying those skills that they felt were most useful in the workplace. There is a fairly common belief among teachers and trainers who have been delivering vocational programmes that employers often have been more interested in the general abilities of prospective employees such as the ability to work with others, to show initiative and to learn new skills than the actual qualification with which they leave full-time education. In the spirit of the Leitch Report that recommended greater levels of engagement of employers in the development of learning programmes, they were invited to help to develop a curriculum that reflected their concerns and one which would enable learners to develop and demonstrate these skills.

So what are these PLTS? Figure 3.3 presents a summary of the main themes and which particular skills are associated with each one and, from this, it may be clearly seen that they are intended to identify aspects of personal development that will enable the learner to become a more rounded and independent individual. As already noted, these have been developed as an important aspect of the 14–19 Diplomas, but there are components of this qualification that might be studied independently of the main programme, as 'stand-alone' qualifications, notably the individual project which carries the value of half an A level, that is 5 credits at level 3 (see Chapter 2 for an explanation of the credit framework). Indeed, at least one university preparing post-graduate trainees for teaching has focused on developing PLTS as a component of the general curriculum. So we can, perhaps, expect to see further developments in this area.

Creative thinkers
a)   Generate ideas and explore possibilities
b)   Ask questions to extend thinking
c)   Connect their own and others' ideas and experiences in inventive ways
d)   Question their own and others' assumptions
e)   Try out alternative or new solutions and follow ideas through
f)   Adapt ideas as circumstances change

Independent enquirers
a)   Identify questions to answer and problems to resolve
b)   Plan and carry out research, appreciating the consequences of decisions
c)   Explore issues, events or problems from different perspectives
d)   Analyse and evaluate information, judging its relevance and value
e)   Consider the influence of circumstances, beliefs and feelings on decisions and events
f)   Support conclusions, using reasoned arguments and evidence

Reflective learners
a)   Assess themselves and others identifying opportunities and achievements
b)   Set goals with success criteria for development and work
c)   Review progress, acting on outcomes
d)   Invite feedback and deal positively with praise, setbacks and criticism
e)   Evaluate experiences and learning to inform future progress
f)   Communicate their learning in relevant ways for different audiences

Team workers
a)   Collaborate with others to work common goals
b)   Reach agreements, managing discussions to achieve results
c)   Adapt behaviour to suit different roles and situations, including leadership roles
d)   Show fairness and consideration to others
e)   Take responsibility, showing confidence in themselves and their contribution
f)   Provide constructive support and feedback to others

Self managers
a)   Seek out challenges or new responsibilities and show flexibility when priorities change
b)   Work towards goals, showing initiative, commitment and perseverance
c)   Organize time and resources, prioritizing actions
d)   Anticipate, take and manage risk
e)   Deal with competing pressures, including personal and work-related demands
f)   Respond positively to change, seeking advice and support when needed
g)   Manage their emotions, and build and maintain relationships

Effective participators
a)   Discuss issues of concern, seeking resolution where needed
b)   Present a persuasive case for action
c)   Propose practical ways forward, breaking these down into manageable steps
d)   Identify improvements that would benefit others as well as themselves
e)   Try to influence others, negotiating and balancing diverse views to reach workable solutions
f)   Act as an advocate for views and beliefs that may differ from your own

Figure 3.3 Summary of Personal Learning and Thinking Skills

Reflection 3.10

Box 3.3 is a case study of a learner researching for her extended project as a part of her Diploma in Sport and Leisure.

Can you identify which aspects of Personal Learning and Thinking Skills that she can provide evidence for in this activity?

Box 3.3 Identifying PLTS in a Diploma Extended Project

Yve is taking the Advanced Diploma in sport and leisure and, with her fellow students, is faced with the challenge of engaging a selected 'specific population' in a sporting activity or active leisure pursuit. Yve persuades her 'team' that women over 55 would be an interesting group to target from the point of view of encouraging active participation. She researches the groups meeting in the local community to find out whom they might approach.

Yve is being instrumental in making her suggestion – she is keen to investigate as preparation for her extended project, which is about the experience of sport in the period since the Second World War and the experience of women in particular. She therefore has an interest in identifying the most appropriate group for her own purposes down the line. For part of her project, she is thinking in terms of a small, oral history enquiry and anticipates that this could accompany the initiative to engage older women in sport and leisure and also be of value to the group in question.

Embedding PLTS in the Sport and Leisure Curriculum

As with Functional Skills, it is intended that PLTS should be fully embedded into the wider curriculum. Indeed, aspects of the 14–19 Diploma curriculum have been specifically developed with this in mind as we can see from Reflection 3.10. But, as has already been discussed in Chapter 2, a main principle of Diploma delivery is learning through Applied Learning strategies such as practical, occupationally relevant activities and also through an assessed work placement. So when planning a curriculum through a scheme of work and lesson plans, it is important to identify opportunities to develop and assess the achievement of PLTS.

> **Reflection 3.11**
>
> The exemplar lesson plan in Figure 3.4, opposite shows how PLTS might be recorded. Note that a code has been used to identify possible opportunities, but you can probably recognize the various PLTs from the initials.
>
> Try to work out which skills are being referred to here and critically review whether or not they are appropriate. Perhaps add some of your own.
>
> Achievement might then be recorded perhaps using one of the useful charts published by the various exam boards.

As an exercise, you might like to try to review the exemplar lesson plan in Chapter 4, Figure 4.4, and try to identify the opportunities for developing and assessing PLTS.

Summary

The Key Skills agenda has its origins in the New Vocationalism movement of the 1980s which sought to promote higher levels of literacy, numeracy and ICT skills in order to develop the economic progress of the UK. We have seen how this has underpinned many programmes of learning since that time and how Key Skills are about to reemerge as Functional Skills.

In this concern for the economic well-being of the nation, we must not underestimate the value to the individual of developing the skills. Not only may this make them more employable, but perhaps it will help them to be more confident in this age where it can be hard to keep up with the rapid growth of technology.

We have identified how people have to overcome barriers to developing their skills: barriers which may have been formed at school or college, or perhaps in their social lives. Some may have special inherent difficulties with learning the skills, and we must be able to identify these and seek out specialist help where necessary. But we must also be aware of our own barriers to the skills and seek to improve our knowledge and understanding of them.

Here we have tried to show how we can make the development of the skills more meaningful by contextualizing them, embedding them into our curriculum, so that the learners are not just going over the same old Maths and English that they did at school, but really see that the skills can have a purpose in their everyday working lives. This is why we now talk about 'Functional Skills': they are skills that we can really use and actually need in order to develop in our chosen occupation.

The next chapter is concerned with developing strategies for effective learning. Arguably, effective learning is underpinned by a certain level of proficiency in the Key and Functional Skills and, as teachers, we need to be able to recognize where our learners may be struggling with these skills and to be able support them so that they can gain higher levels of satisfaction from the learning experience.

Lesson Plan – Designing of equipment

Module	2.3 Science in sport and leisure	Time	3 hours
Class		Date	
Level		No of students:	10

I.L.O	To understand how to evaluate effectively
	To research into current equipment already on the market to help performance
	To design a new piece of equipment to help improve sporting performance for a specific skill

Resources	Internet, computer, colouring pencils, paper

Time	Activity	Student activity	Differentiation	Dip Focus	PLTS
5 minutes	Introduction	What this project consists of. What the ILOs are for this lesson. How you are going to achieve them?			
30 minutes	Starter / Review from last week	Using the information sheet you were provided for home work write a report on each piece of equipment. Try to include diagrams where possible	Students can lay out their report how they like.		
30 minutes	Sport selection for project	Write an introductory page stating which sport you are going to focus upon and why. State 5 skills which you have to perform during that activity. Explain how each skill is performed step by step. Which skill you would be focusing upon when designing your piece of equipment.	Students can lay out their report how they like. Amount of teacher input will vary depending on the student	2.3.1 2.3.2	
30 minutes	Provisional design of equipment	Create a provisional design for your piece of equipment. You must write an explanation on how it will work. Safety considerations, which muscles will it work, the range of motions it will work, where the force will be applied on the body, which pivot points in the body are being used.	Students' design ideas will vary depending on the sport skill they have chosen. The way they go about designing it is entirely up to them – paper or computer	2.3.1 2.3.2 2.3.3 2.3.5 2.3.6	CT a, b, c IE a, b, c, d, f SM b, c, d, g
25 minutes	Discussion	Teacher to split the group in small focus groups. Each group to discuss their ideas for each machine. Students to write notes from the feedback about their design. This will get some ideas to direct the questionnaire.	Amount of teacher input will vary depending on the group. Outcomes of the discussion	2.3.1 2.3.2 2.3.3 2.3.5	IE d RL d, e TW a, d, f SM g EP c, f
1 hour	Questionnaire	Design a questionnaire based upon your design. Your aim is to find out what peers think of your design and later act upon their views. Get 3 peers to evaluate your design.	Students can lay out their questionnaire how they like. Amount of teacher input will vary depending on the student		IE d RL d, e SM g

Figure 3.4 Embedding Personal Learning and Thinking Skills into the Sport and Leisure lesson plan

4

Learning and teaching strategies

At the end of this chapter the reader should be able to:

- Identify the diversity of learners to be found in the lifelong learning sector who might wish to study Sport and Leisure as a vocational subject
- Identify the needs and aspirations of these different groups of learners
- Define the characteristics of effective learning in the context of the Sport and Leisure curriculum
- Develop strategies that will promote effective learning in this context
- Design and plan lessons in Sport and Leisure studies that will promote effective learning

Introduction

We saw in Chapter 2 how the objectives and design of the many varied programmes on offer to the would-be student of Sport and Leisure reflect some very specific philosophies or ideologies of education. We also saw how these, in turn, can influence the way in which the subject might be studied or taught. If we wish to train someone to manage a booking system for a fitness club or leisure centre efficiently, then we need to design a programme that will enable them to develop the necessary techniques on which the system is based. But working in the Sport and Leisure industry demands so much more: by definition, it is a volatile environment in which individuals are physically challenged and in which people interact with each other. The potential for injury and confrontation is always present, and operators working in any given area at any level must be prepared at any time to ensure the Health and Safety of their clients. Clearly this requires so much more than mere technical skills: it will require alertness; an understanding of clients' needs and expectations; intuition to avert potentially dangerous situations, and knowledge and understanding of the limitations and potential of the human body, at the very least.

How can we effectively help learners to develop such techniques, knowledge and understanding? To what extent do we need to consider the different life-experiences, ages and aspirations of the learners themselves when designing our learning programmes?

This is the very essence of this chapter which will first review the nature of the wide variety of learners to be found in the lifelong learning sector as discussed in Chapter 1; then, considering the objectives of the different learning programmes in Sport and Leisure, we will suggest appropriate strategies and methods to promote effective learning; this will lead us to develop lesson plans that will enable us to create meaningful learning experiences.

Learners in the lifelong learning (14+) sector: who are our learners?

In Chapter 1, we considered the nature and expectations of the younger adult compared with the mature adult. Bearing in mind the 'cautionary note' about generalizations, we can briefly summarize these characteristics. Many of our young adults, having experienced the modern PE curriculum, will come to us with at least some skills, knowledge and understanding relevant to the Sport and Leisure curriculum; possibly they will have unrealistic expectations of what is achievable and this against a background of adolescent behavioural development. On the other hand, it is normally expected that the more mature learner will have determined the career path that they wish to follow, will have carefully chosen their programme of study and will have more realistic expectations.

Malcolm Knowles, in his work on the adult learner (1984), identified their characteristics and Table 4.1 provides a useful comparison with younger learners. He went on to suggest that such differences require different approaches to learning and teaching and described the approach to be taken with adults as andragogical, as opposed to how we might plan to teach younger learners who are either still a part of the compulsory education phase, or within two or three years of this, which would be pedagogical.

Table 4.1 The assumptions of andragogy

	Pedagogical	Andragogical
Concept of the learner	Dependent personality	Increasingly self-directed
Role of the learner's experience	To be built on, more than used a resource	A rich resource for learning by self and other
Reading to learn	Uniform by age, level and curriculum	Develops from life tasks and problems
Orientation to learning	Subject-centred	Task or problem-centred
Motivation	By external rewards and punishments	By internal incentives and curiosity

Source: Armitage et al. (2007: 76).

> **Reflection 4.1**
>
> Using Table 4.1, with reference to Knowles' ideas, how might you introduce a CSLA lesson on leading an activity session for a group of children, to a class of 16-year-olds?
>
> How would your approach differ for a class of more mature adults with a variety of experiences?

Knowles' work has been much criticized since he applied his ideas only to adults, and he himself eventually acknowledged that his andragogical approach might be appropriate for all learners: it will become clear from our preferred approaches to teaching and learning that we would concur with this latter view.

Identifying learner needs: learning styles and personalized learning

Every Child Matters

The Every Child Matters agenda was briefly mentioned in Chapter 1, but it is an agenda that has had a huge impact on the school environment and, therefore, is one that we must consider at least for our 14–16 learners. Indeed, it has found credibility in many institutes of post-compulsory education as 'Every Learner Matters'.

Formulated as a Green Paper in 2003, it proposed five main objectives for every child: being healthy, staying safe, enjoying and achieving, making a positive contribution and economic well-being. However, it is the focus on achievement by the individual that has had considerable impact on the curriculum, particularly on the development of the notion of personalized learning.

You can find out more about Every Child Matters on the DCFS website, www.dcsf.gov.uk/everychildmatters, but what, then, does it mean to 'personalize learning'? One thing it doesn't mean is that the teacher needs to plan a separate lesson for each learner in her class! That would surely lead to the road to disillusionment for the teacher:

> [W]hile meeting everyone's needs sounds compassionate and learner-centred it is pedagogically unsound and psychologically demoralizing. The teacher knows that clinging to this assumption will only cause her to carry around a permanent burden of guilt at her inability to live up to this impossible task.
>
> (Brookfield 1998: 133)

What we do mean by personalized learning is that we first acknowledge that each of our learners has had different life experiences and may learn in ways that are different from others. As effective teachers of Sport and Leisure we try to remain aware of this and respond to individual learners appropriately. So what are these differences that our learners may bring to the classroom?

We have already considered some of these in Chapter 1 and in the discussion above, where we noted the differences between young and mature learners. Chapter 3 focused on levels of ability in the Key and Functional Skills and on barriers to learning. So, to plan effective learning activities, we need to make judgements about their needs. Clearly, in the first instance we might generalize their expectations from the type of programme on which they have enrolled. As already discussed, this would range from level 1 introductory programmes, to highly technical, advanced professional qualifications. In turn, the approach that we would take would be very different for each group of learners. We would also take into account their different ages and experiences. As we have seen above, someone who has been a regular gym user themselves for a number of years would probably have very clear ideas on how to conduct an induction session compared to a young if enthusiastic learner relatively new to the training environment.

Learning styles

However, there is more to personalizing learning than referring to these very simplistic categories. Many theorists and researchers have suggested that people prefer to learn in different ways: that they have preferred 'learning styles'. In all, Coffield et al. (2004) have identified 71 different 'learning styles inventories' which are supposed to categorize learners according to their preferred ways of learning. In their highly critical work they claim that, out of all these inventories, just 13 may be classified as 'major models'. The two that appear to be most frequently referred to in Initial Teacher Training are Honey and Mumford's, which has a strong affinity to Kolb's Experiential Learning Model, and the VARK inventory which identifies preferences for Visual, Auditory, Read-write or Kinaesthetic learning.

Harkin et al. (2001: 43) show the Honey and Mumford–Kolb relationship very clearly and we shall revisit the experiential learning model later (Figure 4.1), but the well-known inventory identifies learners as 'Activists', 'Reflectors', 'Theorists' or 'Pragmatists'. For a full commentary on these styles there is ample literature, from the original Honey and Mumford *Manual of Learning Styles* (1992) to Harkin et al. referred to above, but in general the terms are self-explanatory. Some people prefer an active learning style, others are, perhaps, more reflective or prefer to theorize, while still others might take a more practical outlook to their learning.

The VARK model, developed by Flemming (2001), suggests that preferences are related to sensory factors and this simple model is probably the one that is most commonly found in schools and colleges. The initial assessment is simple to administer, and it is relatively easy to embed learning activities to cater for these different preferences into a lesson plan: it is, therefore, a very convenient model to adopt.

However, Coffield et al. (2004) are highly critical of the inventories that are designed to categorize learners. First, on the grounds that the tests seem to be highly subjective and often lacking in reliability and validity and, second, that they tend to stereotype learners, leading to the ever-present danger of our old enemy, the 'self-fulfilling prophesy'.

Whether we can claim that any one student learns better in one way or another or not, it would seem that what we can learn from this is that there are different ways of learning and that by incorporating them all into our lessons, we can ensure that each learner will find a way to engage in the lesson and that, by doing so, we are reinforcing learning in a different way to the benefit of all our learners. This is an important principle that we shall review when it comes to lesson planning later in the chapter.

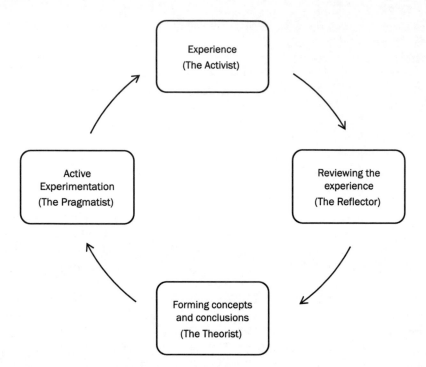

Figure 4.1 Honey and Mumford's Learning Styles related to Kolb's Experiential Learning Model
Source: After Harkin et al. (2001: 43)

Reflection 4.2

Review the lesson plan in Chapter 3 (Figure 3.4).

Bearing in mind the different learning styles mentioned above, how many different ways of learning can you identify in this lesson?

Developing effective learning in the Sport and Leisure curriculum

Chapter 2 examined the various curricula available to our learners so you should be familiar with the subject matter with which they will be required to engage. This could range from simply identifying the bones in the body to analysing the biomechanics of a gymnastic movement, or from simple customer service practice to reviewing the social mix of attendees at a local leisure centre. Clearly the approach one would take for different topics would vary accordingly.

The types of knowledge and skills required for these different topics have been analysed by philosophers and educationists for centuries, but one succinct 'taxonomy' that has proved to be popular and with which you may already be familiar, is that proposed by Bloom. Knowledge was identified under three basic 'domains of learning': cognitive, affective and psychomotor. Table 4.2 shows the characteristics

Table 4.2 Major categories in each of Bloom's Domains of Learning

Cognitive domain	Affective domain	Psychomotor domain
Evaluation	Characterizing	Naturalization
Synthesis	Organizing	Articulation
Analysis	Valuing	Precision
Application	Responding	Manipulation
Comprehension	Receiving	Imitation
Knowledge		

Note: This shows the increasing degrees of difficulty in each of the domains from the bottom (least difficult) to the top.
Source: After Reece and Walker (2007: 54–56).

of each domain: the importance for our planning is that it raises our awareness and helps us to plan ways of developing learning in each domain.

However, the one thing that most topics in the Sport and Leisure curriculum have in common is that they are grounded in practical experience and that provides us with unique opportunities to develop a meaningful learning environment.

Ways of learning – what makes learning effective?

'Making teaching work is all about making learning happen.' So say Phil Race and Ruth Pickford (2007) and the gist of what follows tries suggest ways in which we, as teachers of Sport and Leisure, can enable that.

If we want our learners, whoever they are, to be actively engaged in an effective learning process, we need to examine the principles that underpin that process so that we ensure that our planning takes those principles into account.

The first and most obvious question to ask appears to be, 'What does it mean to learn something?' This is not necessarily a simple question to answer. Do we mean that the learner merely has to memorize facts and regurgitate them at some future date when questioned, say, in an examination? Or does it mean that they should be able to make sense of the information so that they can make use of it in an appropriate situation? These are the kinds of questions that educationsts have wrestled with for centuries and which have led to the rise of many theories of learning. Here we will visit them briefly in an attempt to show how they might each influence the way we teach and plan for teaching.

The Behaviourist school of learning

Returning to our first simple example above, we might recognize this as having elements of a fairly traditional approach to learning and teaching where the teacher is the fount of all knowledge who will pass this on to the learner who, having no knowledge of the subject (the Tabula Rasa), will be filled with what the teacher has selected as 'really useful knowledge'. Paulo Freire (1970), the revolutionary Brazilian educator, described this as 'banking education': the teacher being the 'bank of knowledge' topping up the learner's knowledge account. The advantage of this way of teaching is that it can easily be tested. Thus, learning 'behaviour', such as memorizing facts, can be measured in a way that will satisfy the 'Behaviourist' school of learning theorists. This may well have its uses when learning important data, but has serious limitations: it might help us to remember the names of the muscles in the human body, but tells us little about the theories of how they work or how we can train athletes to analyse and maximize their performance.

The Cognitivist school of learning

The Cognitivist school of learning theory, on the other hand, believes that learning is a developmental process of the intellect and that, therefore, learning should be structured to lead the learner from existing knowledge to new knowledge. Clearly this too has implications for how we plan our lessons: a lesson on comparative training methods, for example, might well begin with asking learners to recall how they might have trained for their various sporting activities and to share this with the rest of the group, comparing their experiences.

The Humanist school of learning

Both of the above theories assume that the teacher makes all the decisions and is central to the learning process. But, yet another movement developed during the twentieth century and became a major contributor to the field of education. This was the Humanist approach which values what learners bring to the learning environment and places them firmly at the centre of the process. The interaction between the teacher and the learner is essential, and this approach has generated a number of methods and strategies to foster or 'facilitate' learning. John Dewey (1963, 1974, in Harkin et al. 2001: 37–8) was a pioneer of these approaches which led initially to the development of 'project methods' that have influenced the Primary School curriculum for decades, but which have also underpinned the coursework-based approach designed to encourage learner-centred research as favoured by BTEC and the National Diploma programmes. We will examine more of these as particularly appropriate ways for learning in Sport and Leisure.

Reflection 4.3

In Chapter 2, Figure 2.2, one of the learning outcomes in a module on health and well-being is: 'Understand the importance of lifestyle factors in the maintenance of health and wellbeing.'

Look up the unit content for this outcome and decide how you might teach this according to each of the learning theories: Behaviourist, Cognitivist and Humanist.

Which would be the most effective way?

For the Behaviourist style you might have decided to present a list of the factors to your class and ask them to learn them in preparation for a test, while the Cognitive approach would see you analysing each factor and structuring the learning around question and answer strategies. The Humanist, however, would certainly engage the class in question and answer perhaps to introduce the topic and to stimulate responses from the learners who would then be set tasks to identify and research the factors in some depth and to come up with recommendations for the maintenance of healthy living. Which do you think would have the greatest impact on the learners?

Deep and surface learning

Ways of learning that stimulate learners to learn independently of the teacher, to research information, to analyse and solve complex problems lead to 'deep learning' that is more meaningful and long-lasting. Conversely, those which demand that they merely learn facts in order to pass a test or examination, facts which might just as easily be forgotten, are thought to encourage only 'surface learning' (Gibbs 1992). Table 4.3 illustrates the comparative characteristics of deep and surface learning.

If we are to achieve deep learning with our learners, which does seem to be the preferable option, then there are clearly implications for the way in which we plan and organize the learning experience.

Graham Gibbs himself suggested a range of teaching strategies and methods which can foster deep learning, including: independent learning, problem-based learning, reflection, group work, learning by doing and project work (Gibbs 1992, in Harkin et al. 2001: 49). Some of these we shall revisit in more detail later.

Unfortunately, all too often, even with activities that appear to be designed to encourage a deep, investigative approach such as research assignments, 'students today commonly adopt surface learning. This is an understandable response to a teaching environment which fails to encourage them to adopt a deep approach' (Race and Pickford 2007: 22). That is, rather than developing their own strategies to solve problems set by the teacher, they will seek ways to come up with the 'right answer', in some cases aided by the teacher who might create a formula or task book

Table 4.3 The characteristics of deep and surface learning

Surface learning	Deep learning
Intention to recall and reproduce lecture notes	Relating concepts to existing knowledge and understanding and to everyday life
Sole aim to pass assessments	Organizing and structuring new information
Passively accepting teacher's ideas or notes	An interest in understanding new materials
No reflection	Challenging new concepts and reading widely
No concept of overall patterns or themes	Examining the logic of the development
Treating assignments as a burden	Determining what is significant

Source: As summarized by Reece and Walker (2007: 78–79).

to ensure that they do. In an environment where institutions, colleges and schools, are judged by results, this is a very tempting option.

You can find out more about these 'theories of learning' from any text on learning and teaching such as Armitage et al. (2007), *Teaching and Training in Post-Compulsory Education*; Capel et al. (2009), *Learning to Teach in the Secondary School*; and Geff Petty's *Teaching Today: A Practical Guide* (2009).

How can we make learning more effective?

So what have we learnt about effective learning from the above? Different theorists have had different ideas about this, but if we are to engage our learners in activities that will lead to meaningful learning experiences and, therefore, deep learning that will have a lasting value, it would seem that they need to be active rather than passive learners. As we have seen, the Sport and Leisure curriculum offers unique opportunities for developing such learning environments, so we can consider two theories that have been particularly influential during the twentieth century.

Experiential learning

We have seen that to stimulate 'deep learning' the learner must be actively engaged in the process of learning. It would seem to be obvious that, central to this approach, is the experience that the learner brings to the dialogue.

One of the most influential educationalists of the century was undoubtedly John Dewey. As an acknowledged Pragmatist and political philosopher, his argument was that: 'learning rests on a mode of life where reason is exercised through problem solving, where the individual participates and contributes to the collective good of society and in the process constitutes their own development' (Olson, in Fegas and Nicoll 2008: 44).

Thus, his views on the value and continuity of experience have informed a number of others who have developed this notion of 'Experiential Learning'. Kolb (1984), building on the work of Kurt Lewin, developed a model, based on Dewey's proposition of internal and external experience, which has provided the basis for the planning of programmes adopting experiential learning methods. We have already looked at Kolb's model in relation to Honey and Mumford's learning styles (see Figure 4.1). The model is cyclical, meaning that each phase leads to the next and the learning is, therefore, a continuous process. The learner begins with knowledge and experience already gained (concrete experience) and, after reflection and experimentation with new ideas, leads to further experience. How does this work in practice?

Reflection 4.4

In a lesson on fitness testing, we want our learners to evaluate the effectiveness of a range of simple tests, such as the standing long jump, body fat composition using skin-fold calipers and a timed 30 metre run.

Using the experiential learning cycle, how might you approach this lesson?

What would be the benefits of experiential learning in this case?

Social learning

It might be noted that Olson's view on Dewey's proposition implies that meaningful learning takes place in a social context. Again, this is a theme that has been taken up and developed by others: Bandura (1969) and Vygotsky saw that while learners brought their own wealth of 'internal knowledge' to the learning environment, this would be developed by others more knowledgeable, such as the teacher or even learner-peers who bring 'external knowledge' to the situation. This element of development through shared knowledge Vygotsky described as the Zone of Proximal Development (1978) and many readers of the psychology of sport will already be familiar with Bandura's theories on social learning which acknowledges similar processes of learning.

So what are the implications for us as teachers of Sport and Leisure? Surely this means that learning is not something that happens in isolation, but that it happens through shared experiences. Strategies that enable this sharing of experience, then, will perhaps contribute towards more effective learning.

Developing expert learners through facilitative approaches

The experts are very good at telling us how they think learning takes place and, to be fair, most of them have worked experimentally to test out their theories. Dewey, for example, set up an experimental school at the University of Chicago where he developed practices that have influenced teaching throughout the twentieth century and now beyond, opening up his classrooms to create social learning spaces where learners might engage in co-operative, investigative, experiential learning involving projects that crossed subject boundaries.

What kinds of strategies and methods can we employ to develop not only our learners' knowledge of Sport and Leisure but also their capacity to learn? We have seen that there does seem to be a general consensus that to be truly effective interactive, experiential learning approaches are important. So what kinds of specific approaches are available to us?

Susan Wallace (2005) distinguishes between strategies and methods and this would seem to be helpful. Strategies generally refer to an overall approach to an activity such as whether the class will engage in group work or individual research and study, or whether they will work together as whole class. The methods would refer to the learning activity itself. For example, the class might be divided into small groups (a strategy) to prepare for a role play, or to research a topic for presentation (methods). On the other hand, the topic might be one that would benefit from whole class engagement (a strategy) in a discussion (a method). The strategy, then, refers to the organization of the activity, whereas the method describes how the learners will engage in learning within that strategy.

Reflection 4.5

If a group visit to a local private health club is a teaching strategy, what learning methods might you employ to ensure that the learners made the most of the opportunity?

It would be helpful, of course, to first define what the purpose of the visit is.

The choice of strategies and methods, as we have seen, will depend on the topic to be studied and possibly the level, but, almost certainly, the nature of the group, relationships within the group, their prior experiences and their preferred way of learning. For example, not all groups by any means will willingly engage in role play activities.

Briefly, here are some methods employing experiential and interactive, social learning strategies that you might use to develop effective learning.

Some interactive learning activities

Discussion

As an introduction to a lesson, discussion can be an indispensable way of immediately engaging learners interactively perhaps finding out what they already know about a new topic or recalling one which you are continuing from a previous session.

Simulation, role play, games and case studies

These are all methods that appear to be very similar and may often be confused but, basically, they are ways in which learners can engage interactively through creating realistic, experiential situations in the classroom. David Jaques and Gilly Salmon in their comprehensive text *Learning in Groups* (2007: 140–1) give the following accounts:

'*Simulations* are working representations of reality. [They are set in] a specific context or scenario . . . They allow students to explore social or physical systems where the real things are too expensive, complex, dangerous, fast or slow for teaching purposes.' For example, dealing with an injury in a given sports situation where an 'actor' would feign an injury to which other students would have to react. Clearly, one would hope that they might never have to actually experience this, but they must be prepared.

'*Role Play* involves people imagining that they are either themselves or someone else in a particular situation. They are asked to behave as they feel that person would, and to try behaviours that may not normally be a part of their repertoire.'

Reflection 4.6

Consider the role play scenario in Box 4.1:

- How would you manage this in your lesson?
- What problems can you foresee?
- How would you improve it?

LEARNING AND TEACHING STRATEGIES

Box 4.1 Role play scenario for a sports development course

Student 1

You are a football/netball coach supporting your team on the sidelines. There are one or two parents standing near you. A challenge goes unnoticed by the referee/umpire. You have to keep calm and also calm down parents who may over-react.

Student 2

You are a parent watching your son/daughter in a football/netball match against a team that is always considered to be rather physical. A challenge goes unnoticed by the referee/umpire and you react by shouting at the official.

Between you the situation must be resolved.

'*Games* [are] group exercises in which players cooperate or compete towards a given end within a regime of specific rules. Players behave as themselves.' Two groups of students on a community sports development course, for example, might be given the task to design a holiday activity programme for 9–11-year-old children which is offered, in competition with each other, for tender to a local authority. The outcome could be decided from presentations to a selected panel of experts.

'*Case studies* are descriptions of a possible real-life event presented in order to illustrate special and/or general characteristics of a problem.' Given the role play in Box 4.1 as a case study, students could be asked to discuss possible solutions to the problem without actually acting it out.

Clearly, the case study could form the basis of role play scenario, and elements of the game example are either a simulation or role play. As Jaques and Salmon point out, 'All of these definitions are a matter of degree and balance – combinations abound.' The differences are probably not too important, but as ways of experiencing the realities of working environments in different ways to different degrees, they are invaluable. However, as always, it is of utmost importance that the exercise should be contextualized in the learning environment through careful preparation and followed by debrief and feedback. In fact, some role play events can become very fraught and passions can run high as learners get into role: on such occasions the debrief is most necessary to bring the learners back to their reality.

Applied Learning

The term Applied Learning is widely used now to describe activities that relate directly to occupational roles. Most of the above will provide opportunities to develop such activities but, of course, much learning in the Sport and Leisure curriculum is best experienced through practical activity either directly in the workplace or through simulation or role play. The NVQ for Coaching and Instructing, for example, would be meaningless unless the learner could actually practise, say, taking a football coaching session with a group of their peers, or leading a colleague through a gym induction session.

Making the most of educational visits and work placements

Of course, there is nothing quite like experiencing the real working environment to capture the full flavour of the Sport and Leisure industry.

Visits to sporting venues, for example, preferably supported by a talk and/or a guided tour by an expert practitioner with time for questions will be invaluable in placing the theoretical activities of the classroom into the context of the realities of the workplace. However, such visits will require in-depth planning to prepare learners for the experience so that they can make the most of it. Worksheets and questionnaires will help to focus their enquiries on relevant information. Trawling the internet will give them an insight, and group discussion may help to refine their research. Subsequently the visit should be followed up perhaps with an assignment and/or group presentations in order, again, to consolidate learning. Examples of these activities will be found in Chapters 5 and 6 where we will consider assessment methods such as assignments and resources that include the workplace.

Work placements do, of course, give learners first-hand experience of working in the industry. However, again, this should not be regarded as a one-off experience unrelated to classroom activity. There should be careful preparation through discussion and research prior to the experience so that learners have some idea of what to expect, with research to carry out while in placement, identifying important aspects of the industry and its working practices. Worksheets might be appropriate, but perhaps a journal with daily activities might be more useful. Chapter 6 develops the idea of using the work placement as a resource further.

Preparing for effective learning in the Sport and Leisure lesson

Having considered the various factors that can stimulate and affect learning and strategies and methods, we now need to consider what this all means when confronted by a class of eager (or perhaps even not so eager!) learners. After all, ensuring that our learners are actually benefitting from our lessons is very important.

Preparing the learning environment

One of the first things we need to consider is the often neglected learning environment. Abraham Maslow in his seminal and very well-known work on the 'hierarchy of needs' would say that, unless the environment is comfortable (both physically and psychologically) and stimulating, very little learning could take place. Although his work was aimed at business and industrial environments, Figure 4.2 shows how his ideas might be interpreted for the classroom.

Even the layout of the desks or working spaces in a classroom can make a statement about the teacher's intentions and have a major impact on the learners' expectations as they enter the room.

Figure 4.2 Maslow's hierarchy of needs adapted for teachers of young adults
Source: Harkin et al. (2001: 62).

Reflection 4.7

What kind of teaching activity would rows of desks suggest to you? Conversely, what about the horseshoe layout or blocks of three or four tables forming a wider working space?

But we can make assumptions about each of these layouts. If we recall the discussion on learning styles, it is possible that some students may feel that they respond better to the 'lecture room' layout and, for a university lecture in a tiered lecture hall with perhaps 60 plus students, what alternatives are there?

The rationale for the horseshoe layout is that it brings the teacher closer to the learners enabling better eye-contact and helps to include everyone into the group. However, discussion with some adult learners revealed that they felt 'exposed' and psychologically uncomfortable in this arrangement and preferred a layout where they could sit behind other people. How many of us, given the option, sit in the front row at a lecture?

Working around grouped tables, however, suggests interactive learning and presents the opportunity for small group work, although it can present problems where the focus of the session needs to be centralized, perhaps focused on the teacher.

As we have already suggested, such issues are not set in stone but will be determined by the nature of the group, their preferred way of learning and, perhaps, the subject and the context. Certainly, many of our learners in the Sport and Leisure curriculum will have high expectations that the learning will be largely of a practical, applied learning nature, and many sessions are undoubtedly best taught in the sports environments of the playing field, leisure centre or fitness gym. These are, after all, the environments in which many of the activities that form the basis of their occupational roles will take place in any case.

Reflection 4.8

You have to take a class on the principles of fitness in a temporary classroom with no electronic resources. How would you set the scene for your learners to make the environment more inviting and stimulate their interest on arrival?

We will assume that you have access to the room for, say, half an hour before the lesson (which, as experienced teachers will know, is by no means usually guaranteed!).

What does the Sport and Leisure lesson plan look like?

In Chapter 2 we looked at the scheme of work as the mid- to long-term planning process of our curriculum and briefly discussed the role of the lesson plan as the preparation for putting the scheme into action.

Good planning is essential if we are to make the most of time we have with our students and ensure that the learning is effective.

A well-designed lesson plan will:

- make clear exactly what it is you want your students to learn.
- structure activities that will enable them to achieve this, bearing in mind the opportunities that the topic provides to stimulate learning and also the profiles of the learners as discussed previously in this chapter.
- identify ways that you can assess whether they are achieving your lesson aims both throughout the lesson and at the end.
- show how learning might be stimulated and supported by the use of appropriate resources.

The plan will also provide a good point of reference throughout the lesson to ensure that you are working within the given time frame and towards your proposed objectives.

Surely the committed teacher must begin by asking themselves several important questions. The first must be to clearly identify what they want their students to learn from the experience and why this is important: this would be the aim of the lesson. Having established this, they should ask how they would know that they had achieved this aim: this will help to identify not only the lesson objectives but also ways that learning activities should be organized in order to achieve them and how to assess whether they had or not. Finally, they should consider which resources would help them to achieve the aim.

Concerned that students at university generally seemed to engage in surface learning (just sufficient to pass exams and gain a degree), John Biggs (2003) analysed the learning situation and presented it in a way that he termed 'constructive alignment'.

Figure 4.3 is an adaptation of his more sophisticated model but clearly shows how learning, which is central to all our activities here, is first predefined by our objectives or what it is that we would like our learners to learn, and that meaning is constructed through the arrangement of 'appropriate learning activities'. This leads us back to the question of how we would know just what the learners take away from the experience.

The process of planning, therefore, begins by identifying what the lesson is all about: the aim. In the case of the lesson plan in Figure 4.4, the aim, although not specifically stated as such, is probably 'To understand the make-up of the human skeleton.' This may seem to be rather vague and use of the word 'understand' is often criticized in this context: perhaps 'to learn about the structure of the human skeleton' might be more appropriate. It still seems very general, but this is the nature of an aim. As Geoff Petty observes, 'Aims are like compass directions, indicating the general direction in which the teacher wishes to travel.' These are often taken from the awarding body specifications and are a guide as to the detail of the objectives, or intended learning outcomes, which are the means by which we can arrive at the destination or

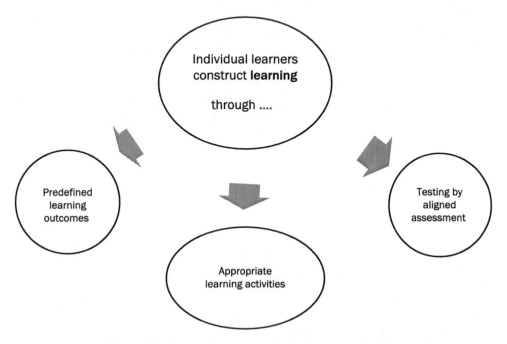

Figure 4.3 A model for constructive alignment of learning

Lesson Plan – Bones and Joints

Module	2.3 Science in sport and leisure		Time	3 hours
Class			Date	
Level	2		No of students:	10

I.L.O	To understand the make up of the human skeletal system To know the categories of joints To identify the 6 types of synovial joint

Resources	PowerPoint presentation, Human body parts sheet, plain paper, scissors, glue, colouring pencils, relevant books, computers, internet, interactive whiteboard

Time	Activity	Student activity	Differentiation	Dip Focus	PLTS
5 minutes	Introduction	What this unit consists of. What the ILOs are for this lesson. How you are going to achieve them.			
25 minutes	Make up the human skeleton	Cut out the skeleton parts carefully. Stick them in the correct place on the paper provided	WT – Provide students with skeleton diagram WB – allow student to draw the skeleton	2.3.1	
15 minutes	Label the skeleton correctly	Label the following bones **Skull (Cranium), Scapular, Humerus, Vertebrae, Pelvis, Patella, Tibia, Fibula, Femur, Ulna, Radius, Ribs, Sternum, Clavicle**	Students can use either books or the internet to find out the correct location WT – Put diagram up on board	2.3.1	IEb IEd
5 minutes	Marking of the skeleton	Students to peer mark the skeleton diagram. They must tick the correct label and mark a cross where incorrect. Teacher to put up the correct diagram on the board. Must be neat when marking	N/A	2.3.1	
10 minutes	Axial and Apendicular skeleton	Choose two colours. Colour the axial skeleton in one colour. And the apendicular in the other	Students can use either books or the internet to find out the correct location WT – Put diagram up on board	2.3.1	IEb IEd
10 minutes	Spine diagram	Students to colour in the 5 sections of the spine correctly – ensure that the correct number of vertebrae are coloured in. Each section is to be labelled with the number of vertebrae in brackets	Students can use either books or the internet to find out the correct number WT – Put diagram up on board	2.3.1	IEb IEd

Time	Topic	Activity	Differentiation	Ref	Skills
15 minutes	Foot and hand structure	Students to use the internet to seek a picture of the structure of the hand and foot. It must be labelled.	WT – Provide students with website WB – allow student to draw and label own diagram	2.3.1	IEb IEd
10 minutes	Revision time	Students to revise what they have just produced for the end of session quiz	Students may revise by their own means – either on own or in small groups		
20 minutes	3 types of joints Poster Go through the information with them	Students to design a poster based on the 3 categories of joints – • Define what is meant by a joint • They must describe what is meant by fixed, immoveable, slightly moveable joint, provide a location within the body, include a picture for each category of joint	Students can choose to make notes when explaining or they may use the internet / books for the answer	2.3.1	IEb IEd
30 minutes	Synovial Joints Go through the information with them	Students to complete the synovial joints worksheet. • Task 1: They must state the location for these types of joint. Choose one location and state which bones meet here. Explain the range of motion at each. Provide 3 sporting examples • Task 2: They must describe what each type of movement is, provide 3 sporting examples. Finally they must state the opposite action	Students can choose to make notes when explaining or they may use the internet / books for the answer	2.3.1	IEb IEd
10 minutes	Revision time	Students to revise what they have just produced for the end of session quiz	Students may revise by their own means – either on own or in small groups		
25 minutes	(Plenary) Bones and joints quiz	Teacher to play the PowerPoint with questions on. Students to answer the questions on the answer sheet. After the quiz is complete – students to swap papers. Teacher to go through the papers marking the answers correctly.	N/A	2.3.1	

Figure 4.4 Exemplar lesson plan

aim. The objectives are how we identify what exactly the learners should have learnt by the end of the lesson. In fact that very phrase is often used on lesson plans and you should be able to place it at the start of each objective: 'At the end of the lesson the learners will know the categories of joints,' for example.

So, if our lesson is to be 'constructively aligned,' we next need to decide upon the learning activities that will enable the learners to achieve the objectives and then, finally, to devise ways of determining how we will know that they have achieved them. This is the subject of Chapter 5, but at this stage we need to note that assessment is integral to the whole learning process.

The role of formative assessment in facilitating learning

Although we shall discuss assessment in Chapter 5, it is appropriate to briefly raise the issue of formative assessment at this point, for this is the on-going assessment throughout the learning experience where the learner can identify what progress they have made, what still needs to be done and which direction to take their learning next.

Reflection 4.9

We considered how the aims and objectives determined the structure of the lesson in Figure 4.4, now carry this analysis a step further and consider the following:

- the sequencing and variety of the activities;
- assessment of learning both throughout the lesson and at the end;
- resources;
- identification of opportunities to develop Key/Functional Skills (see Chapter 3);
- identification of opportunities to achieve PLTS (see Chapter 3);
- planning for differentiated and personalized learning.

Summary

This chapter has been all about the front-line experience of learning and teaching. Whatever the background of the subject and the theories about curriculum, interacting with the learners in the classroom is the ultimate aim of our studies here. So we have tried to understand, first, what our Sport and Leisure learners are likely to want out of the experience: their expectations. If we can analyse that, then perhaps we can identify the best way to teach them.

To help us with this task we have considered a range of theories about what it means to learn something and about how people learn. Our quest has been to try to identify how we create effective learning environments specific to the Sport and Leisure curriculum. The conclusions we hope you will have reached are based on the nature of the subject. The premise on which it is based is, after all, that it is concerned with human physical activity, so active, experiential, applied learning is going to be a major strategy for the teacher of Sport and Leisure.

However, we must not forget that, like most disciplines, this activity is supported by a great deal of academic, theoretical study and that all of our learners will benefit from a deeper understanding of the subject that studies bring at their respective levels. Indeed, some will want to study this theory in great depth. Our challenge then is how to make this meaningful and interesting. I hope that we have addressed this sufficiently for you to be able to develop your own creative strategies which will engage your learners and motivate them in their studies.

Finally, we looked at how you can organize this learning experience in the most effective way and have used the model of 'constructive alignment' as guide. You can look this up in more detail in Biggs and Tang (2007) *Teaching for Quality Learning at University*. But it is important to note the role that assessment plays in the model, and this is the subject of the next chapter.

5

Assessing the Sport and Leisure curriculum

In this chapter we will be looking at:

- What we mean by 'assessment'
- The reasons why we assess
- Different types of assessment
- The ways that different Sport and Leisure programmes are assessed
- The principles of assessment applied to the Sport and Leisure curriculum
- Different methods of assessment used in the Sport and Leisure curriculum
- How to plan an assessment strategy
- How to design assessments for Sport and Leisure

Introduction

So that we are all clear about what this chapter is really about, it might be pertinent to ask the question, 'What is assessment?' In educational circles, it generally means finding out what learners know or can do, and what they have learnt. Armitage and Renwick (2007) would say that it is 'about the judgements of assessors with relation to the quality of student achievement'. The 'assessors', of course, could be any number of people from awarding body examiners, to you, the teacher, or even the learners themselves, as in peer and self-assessment.

Reflection 5.1

Think back to the last two or three times that you were assessed for anything at all: it might be for a coaching award, an examination for a degree, or even a driving test. How many different ways can you remember being assessed? Were they accurate tests of what you had learnt?

In Chapter 4, we showed how assessment must be seen as an important component of the learning process and not as something just tacked onto the end of a course as a measure of whether or not the learner has 'passed' or failed'. If you have studied the acquisition of skill in sport psychology (and kinaesthetic skill is, after all, a type of knowledge: see the earlier references to Bloom's taxonomy), then you will know that analysis of performance, and especially the feedback that follows this, are really how learning takes place. How else would you know whether or not you had learnt something, or how well you had performed? It is by following this process that we can modify our 'behaviour' in a way that leads to improvement.

This is also true for cognitive and affective knowledge. Assessment and feedback are essential to the learning process. It should not be the main objective of your learning programmes, though frequently it is: we would then say that the learning is 'assessment driven', and this would tend to lead to 'surface learning' when the learner only aims to acquire sufficient knowledge to pass the assessment rather than to learn for learning's sake.

Assessment should support and, indeed, enhance learning. Whether it comes at the end of your programmes or at intervals during them, it offers a form of feedback in answer to the question, 'How am I doing?' Such assessment is 'formative' assessment for learning because it supports the development and growth of the learner. By answering this question, we will know whether or not the learner has 'got it' (that is, the knowledge and understanding) and see what needs to be done to help them 'get it'. Assessment that comes as an end test is called 'summative' because it is a test of the sum total of the learner's knowledge and understanding.

In this chapter we will be looking at different forms of assessment used in Sport and Leisure programmes and this might be a good point to refer back to Table 2.1. Morrison and Ridley's matrix shows how different ideologies generate different assessment methodologies, and we can relate this to our various Sport and Leisure programmes. A level Sport Studies, for example, arguably follows the Classical Humanist, elitist, knowledge-based curriculum and is assessed largely by examination, whereas the National Diploma has a more 'Progressive Humanist' agenda favouring coursework-based assessment which requires a formative approach as learners develop their knowledge and understanding through autonomous learning activities. On the other hand, many assessments in Sport and Leisure are outcome-driven and instrumentalist, such as NVQs in which learners have to prove competence by performing tasks successfully.

The merits and appropriateness of each type of assessment will be considered in terms of the principles of validity, authenticity, reliability and practicability, and we will further examine the methods that each employs, with suggestions as to how to design assessment activities that fulfil these criteria.

Finally, we shall look at how you can design your own assignments for coursework and, in the light of the above, we will need to consider the following:

- What constitutes success and how you measure this.
- How this 'journey' is staged in terms of achievement, in a way that is realistic to a learner and acceptable to a curriculum.
- How you convey this information to your learners.

Why do we need to assess our learners?

Reflection 5.2

Referring back to the assessments you identified in Reflection 5.1, why were you assessed? What did the assessment tell you about 'the quality of your achievement'?

Now think about the last time you assessed a group of Sport and Leisure learners, and ask the same questions.

Assessment, then, is how we measure what our learners know and can do or what they have learnt. But why do we need to know this? The following are some good reasons for assessing them:

- *We find out what the learners already know and can do.* As a teacher, it is helpful to know what our learners know before they begin a programme of learning so that we can adapt the plan accordingly: a test which does this would be called 'diagnostic'. This is an essential form of assessment if we are to design 'personalized learning' programmes.

- *We find out what they have learnt from our lessons.* Clearly, this is important information for us to ascertain whether or not our planned teaching has been effective and to modify our plans if necessary. It also serves as a reminder to the learners of what the lesson was all about.

- *We can evaluate our learning programmes.* There are a number of indicators that we can use to measure the success of our programmes, but assessing the outcomes in terms of the quality of student learning is probably the most obvious way.

- *We can monitor learner progress.* Assessment provides a check on what has been learnt and what still needs to be done: which of our learners has 'got it' and which ones need further attention. In this sense, with quality feedback, it becomes 'formative'. It will also tell us whether any of them are ready to progress to higher levels such as HNDs or Foundation degrees.

- *Assessment can motivate our learners.* Knowing that there is a deadline for an assignment or that there is a test or exam coming up is a sure way of motivating learners but, even more important is the inspiration they get from any successful assessment.

- *Assessment provides a public record of the efficacy of the programme.* Naturally any education system needs to measure success, and the success or otherwise of educational establishments and training providers is continually measured in terms of results and grade scales to establish their position in the league tables. This approach has tended to lead to a qualification-driven environment which perhaps overlooks to some extent the benefits to the individual learner and the values that accrue from the learning process itself.

How is Sport and Leisure assessed?

Since the range and type of Sport and Leisure courses are as varied as the types of learners likely to undertake such programmes, you might reasonably expect a different approach to assessment per course type, mode of delivery and even line of learning.

Considering all of this, and taking an 'end product' point of view, it would seem wise to establish some parameters in terms of achievement, in this context, meaning not necessarily cohorts of successful learners measured by the extent of their qualification, more the key knowledge and skills that can be taken away, and critically, for vocational courses, applied to the multitude of Sport and Leisure environments.

So, if not by qualification, then how can we measure this achievement? By what standards do we measure it?

Reflection 5.3

Consider three different assessments that you have experienced as a student of Sport and Leisure (or as a teacher) and try to identify how success was measured.

Was it against a set standard, or against a hypothetical 'average mark'?

What did this tell you about your progress (or your learners' progress)?

Deciding on the standards – referencing

'Referencing' provides us with a framework for designing our programmes because it defines the standard, or reference, against which we measure achievement.

Criterion referencing

The measure here is a criterion: a standard is set, generally by an awarding body, and success is measured by achievement of that standard with no reference to how many learners achieve it. A number of programmes in Sport and Leisure are criterion referenced such as NVQs and National Diplomas.

Figure 5.1 is an example of an NVQ Element from Teaching Coaching and Instructing Sport Activities which identifies specific assessment criteria which the learner must clearly demonstrate before achieving the award. Figure 5.2, on the other hand, shows part of a grading grid for a National Diploma programme in Sport, again with clear criteria for assessment.

The difference to note here is that, whereas the NVQ criteria are simply achieved or not by demonstration, the National Diploma criteria allow for different standards of achievement. This is one of the major areas of debate in the competency assessed curriculum.

Vocational assessment is generally underpinned by the development of practical skills, for example, sports leadership or fitness assessment techniques. Perhaps the

Element D44.3: The candidate must be able to: *Coach participants to improve performance*	
Performance criteria	**Range**
When doing so, the participant must: 1. Observe the participants' performance throughout the session as appropriate to their needs and their level of experience 2. Identify the participants' strengths and weaknesses correctly 3. Use appropriate coaching methods and activities to develop the participants' performance 4. Adapt their plans to respond to the changing needs of the participants during the session and the environment 5. Provide feedback in a clear and positive manner	*This element covers the following types of participants:* a) Individuals b) Groups c) With particular needs as defined by the technical definition of the sport/activity *the following level of experience of:* a) Introductory participants b) Participants with some experience c) Mixed ability group *and the following types of needs:* a) Individual b) Group

Figure 5.1 An NVQ Element of Assessment with criteria

Grading Criteria		
To achieve a **pass** grade the evidence must show that the learner is able to:	To achieve a **merit** grade the evidence must show that, in addition to the pass criteria, the learner is able to:	To achieve a **distinction** grade the evidence must show that, in addition to the pass and merit criteria, the learner is able to:
P1 describe one test for each component of physical fitness, including advantages and disadvantages	M1 explain the advantages and disadvantages of one fitness test for each component of fitness	
P2 prepare an appropriate health screening questionnaire		
P3 devise and use appropriate health screening procedures for two contrasting individuals	M2 describe the strengths and areas for improvement for two contrasting individuals using information from health screening questionnaires and health monitoring tests	D1 Evaluate the health screening questionnaires and health monitoring test results and provide recommendations for lifestyle improvement

Figure 5.2 National Diploma grading grid

best measure of this is assessment of these skills in the workplace, as part of a structured assessment experience for an NVQ programme. The learner, having been shown, may practise, reflect and finally be summatively assessed against the criteria as part of a necessarily longitudinal process.

Norm referencing

While the criterion approach may prove beneficial to the learner, the assessor and potentially the employer, a different approach may be required in considering an assessment protocol that would sufficiently engage a learner seeking to extend knowledge or a deeper understanding of the processes. Often such assessments use examinations or tests in which learners are measured against each other's performance as in A level Sport Studies: this is known as 'norm' referencing because it measures the success of learners against their peers and against what is considered to be the average standard. So about 50 per cent may pass, and 50 per cent may not.

Ipsative assessment

Throughout this publication we have referred to personalized learning and the focus on the development of each individual learner. Ipsative assessment is the way in which we can measure this development because it is self-referenced, that is, it measures an individual's progress from one given point in time to another. A useful analogy is to be found in fitness testing where a client might undertake a test before undertaking an exercise programme. A further test would then measure how much the client had improved.

Ipsative assessment might be used alongside criterion referencing where the learner sets out to achieve a standard and, having achieved this, can identify which standard to work towards next. Although NVQs may be considered somewhat Behaviourist in design, they do also have some 'learner-centred' attributes which allow the participant some measure of autonomy in deciding how best to achieve the award, as the specifications for Teaching, Coaching and Instructing inform us: 'The candidate and assessor should discuss the best way of assessing each element in this unit and plan how it will be done' (SPRITO 1997).

Assessing different Sport and Leisure programmes

Types of summative assessment

So far we have discussed a number of issues concerning purposes and standards, and you may have noticed that this has been contextualized by referring to different types or modes of assessment: exams, coursework and practical demonstration. Before approaching the subject of planning a strategy and designing an assessment, it would be helpful to consider the merits and problems of these modes in a little more depth.

Examinations

Generally, as we have already suggested, exams are norm-referenced forms of assessment that tend to focus on the testing of knowledge: A levels and GCSE would be a typical example. They are tests of knowledge acquired during the course of the programme of learning. That is not to say that these qualifications do not include coursework which may have an element of criterion referencing, but ultimately, we expect a certain percentage to pass and a certain percentage to fail.

Although coursework is a very popular form of assessment, there are many strong arguments for the inclusion of an exam-based system to either partly or wholly replace the coursework-led approach.

Generally exams are more convenient to organize and manage; they can be modified and take less time in terms of development and grading. Exam-based systems can also provide more rigid external validity (see later) and elicit population normative statistics which can form a point of reference or group comparison. In addition, achievement data are easily stored and potentially provide longitudinal comparative performance data.

The key arguments against an exam-based system in vocational learning are that often the greatest value of vocational programmes is the opportunity to provide consistent formative feedback as opposed to this clinical summative approach. In addition, you could question the validity of norm-based referencing as being focused on individual characteristics and situational antecedents as opposed to a true global sample. Critics of this approach could also point to measurement of only shallow learning, and state that criterion-based assessment is in fact more reliable than norm-referenced data, particularly for vocational areas such as Sport and Leisure where practical application should form the root of any assessment method.

Coursework

Coursework generally refers to assignments that are centre-devised measures of performance. It could be practical, theoretical, academic or vocational. In most instances, it is regulated or verified by an awarding body and exists in most Sports and Leisure programmes, including GCSEs, GCE A levels, BTEC Level 2 and Level 3 Diplomas and the 14–19 Diploma.

For many of the traditional qualifications in PE and Sports Studies, coursework exists to test skills that cannot be assessed with any validity with an exam-based system, such as for practical performance assessment in PE coursework. In this setting it is often viewed as being a motivational tool, an opportunity for formative and summative feedback and a useful strategy for those who under-perform in exam environments.

One of the characteristics of coursework assessment is that the summative assessment can be spread across the duration of the course. Consider a BTEC National or First in Sport, where centres design their own assessments. There is encouragement by the awarding body to spread the summative assessment throughout the length of the programme. Similarly NVQ Sport programmes measure competence in a range of skills, such as customer service, which lend themselves to a range of assessment practices, with the focus of an eventual, refined product, for example, being able to competently deal with a customer complaint at a leisure centre reception desk.

In a recent review of coursework, *A Review of GCE and GCSE Coursework*

Arrangements (QCA 2005), there was an endorsement of this approach to assessment in terms of the benefit to learners, and of its general advantages which were seen to outstrip the potential shortcomings. It did, however, also raise some areas of concern.

It suggested that all assessors must authenticate the work of the learners that they assess, effectively providing a professional endorsement, especially where coursework was not completed in the centre. Many centres ask that the learner submitting the work authenticates their own submission, thereby helping to eliminate plagiarism. Attempting to claim the work of another as your own is nothing new, but temptation now exists in a number of different ways, from directly copying from web pages to purchasing coursework from organizations that will produce coursework on demand for a fee. IT and specialized software such as 'Turnitin' are now available that will identify plagiarized submissions.

Since 2007, all teachers and lecturers have been required to register with the General Teaching Council (GTC) or the Institute for Learning (IfL) and evidence of malpractice in this, or any other matter could result in being effectively 'struck off'. In addition, it is possible for awarding bodies to be disqualified from offering a set of qualifications.

However, perhaps the main advantage of coursework and the principal difference between this and exam-based assessment is that it focuses on the processes of learning as much as the content. The learner is expected to analyse the task set and interpret it so that they conduct research and present their findings in the form of the assignment. Throughout the duration of the programme there is a need for regular progress checks that will include feedback given to learners about their progress. Thus, the assessment is, to an extent, also formative not only for the benefit of the learner but also the tutor who is in a position to make regular reviews of their own teaching.

Surprisingly, many learners who decide to follow a coursework-focused programme, often because they are disenchanted by the exam system which has failed them to date, find the process of continuous assessment much more onerous than they thought it would be.

Practical demonstration

Since the focus of Sport and Leisure is inevitably on participation, most programmes will include some form of practical work and, therefore, assessment. This might be related to personal performance as in the practical elements of GCSE or the National Diploma in Excellence in Sport Performance, or to coaching teaching and instructing as in the NVQ.

In the former, assessment might be a one-off performance of ability, but to an extent, it could be ipsative in the sense that performance might be measured diagnostically at the start of the programme, formative since it is monitored throughout and then summative when measured at the end. Coaching, leading and organizing Sport and Leisure activities, however, can be developed in coursework mode throughout the duration of the programme, largely through the practice of leading sessions with other learner peers until a standard is achieved sufficient to satisfy the assessment criteria. Figure 5.1, which we saw earlier, is a summary of NVQ criteria for an element of such a programme.

In fact, many Sport and Leisure programmes now include elements of at least two and perhaps all three modes of assessment. A levels and GCSEs, we have already noted, have practical assessments as well as time-constrained exams, and National Diplomas, traditionally assessed by coursework, now have timed-constrained assignments completed under exam conditions.

Such a system perhaps answers all the criticisms of each type of assessment. Provided that balance is maintained between them: it would ensure the opportunity for academic rigour through the exam; provide opportunities for learner-centred delivery and assessment through the coursework, and enable learners to be assessed on the merits of their practical performance. Perhaps this is only appropriate considering the cross-curricular nature of Sport and Leisure.

Reflection 5.4

Staying with your own experiences of assessment and thinking about examinations, coursework and practical demonstration, which was your preferred option?

Does this depend on what was being assessed?

What were the benefits (and pitfalls) of each method, in your experience?

Planning an assessment strategy

Planning for assessment is a vital part of an aligned approach to planning for learning, as we noted in Chapter 4. In an ideal situation it will involve a number of agencies, potentially including senior management, other teaching staff, industry stakeholders and employers and wherever possible the learners, who are more likely to achieve if they have a stake in their assessment design. A well-planned assessment strategy will identify areas of strengths and weakness and provide a challenging, vocationally relevant assessment plan.

To be meaningful and worthwhile, assessment measures should follow certain rules or principles. Here we visit the accepted principles and try to apply them to our design of Sport and Leisure assessments.

The principles of assessment applied to the Sport and Leisure curriculum

Validity

In short, validity is the fitness for purpose of an assessment tool. Does it accurately measure what it sets out to measure? Primarily this is the role of the awarding body who will seek to ensure this, either in the design of their own externally set assessments or in the moderation of internally centre-set assessment by a process of moderation or verification (see later in this chapter).

Tummons (2007) suggests a differentiation in the types of validity;

- *Face validity* is measured in the way in which an assessment looks like an assessment. In other words, it has academic credibility, free from typographical or grammatical errors, possibly measured against existing or previous similar assessments. A well-written and functional assessment tool with an air of institutional formality is required to meet face validity.

- *Content validity* is measured in terms of how the assessment tool matches the grading specification requirements and the clarity of assessment objectives. In other words, it will accurately reflect the content as set out in specifications and will not ask questions about material that is not included in them.

- *Construct validity* will measure how closely the assessment assesses what the specification says it should measure. Consider a fitness-based unit, and an assessment that requires a learner to physically measure several components of fitness such as body fat percentage or muscular power.

  If the criterion requires that the learner is measured in terms of understanding, handling, and recording fitness test results, then a practical assessment is a better way of testing them than asking them to write an essay about it in an exam. On the other hand, if we wanted to assess their specific knowledge of the components of fitness, then a more formal exam-based system may be more relevant.

- *Predictive validity* is measured in terms of the degree to which predictions based on results can be used to determine future performance and achievement. Learners and providers are frequently asked not only to produce evidence of prior achievement, but also current predicted measures, such as a GCSE candidate who has applied to a local college for a Level 3, National Diploma programme, or that same learner two years down the line who will be making an application to UCAS for an undergraduate degree.

Awarding bodies seek to establish validity by accrediting specifications with the approval of key government agencies such as QCA. As we saw in Chapter 2, recently (2010) all BTEC National and First programmes were reaccredited to embrace the Qualifications and Credit Framework (QCF) and as a result significant alterations to the way in which the programmes were assessed were made. As well as vocational updates, changes were made to the names of the programmes, for example, BTEC Sport programmes previously known as BTEC Nationals and Firsts were re-titled Level 3 Nationals and Level 2 Firsts respectively.

Assessment by awarding bodies of centre-designed assessments and indeed the quality of assessment decisions continues to be measured by a mixture of sampling methods, external quality assessment, moderation, verification and standardization.

Reliability

Assessment is considered reliable if, when applied on a number of occasions, the results produced are consistent. Rather than the focus on how appropriate an assessment tool is (validity), reliability is a measure of how consistent an assessment tool is, as well as its accuracy.

Reliability is measured by awarding bodies by examination or coursework standardization, methods for which will differ according to the assessment tools used.

An exam-led programme such as A Level Physical Education ensures reliability for exams by exam marking through a system of rigorous standardization. Examiners mark a sample of work according to a set marking scheme which is, in turn, submitted to scrutiny at an examiners' meeting, after which their work is carefully monitored by a lead examiner.

Standardization of coursework is achieved in standardization meetings in which moderators debate grade bands and score across a sample of submitted work, before embarking upon the responsibility of moderating assessed grades across a range of centre assessments.

Reflection 5.5

Consider the assignment set in Figure 5.3, opposite.

To what extent do you think it fulfils the principles of validity?

Is it a valid test of the learner's ability to 'understand the impact of stress, arousal and anxiety on performance'?

Can you think of ways that this might be assessed other than the presentation?

Would the presentation be a reliable test of the learner's understanding?

Authenticity

Put simply, this is the suitability of the task. Consider the suitable forms of assessment available to an assessor for the delivery of an NVQ type assessment in fitness testing where a written report would clearly not be suitable, and thus not authentic.

Grant Wiggins offers a definition of authenticity;

Engaging and worthy problems or questions of importance, in which students must use knowledge to fashion performances effectively and creatively. The tasks are either replicas of or analogous to the kinds of problems faced by adult citizens and consumers or professionals in the field.

(Wiggins 1993: 229)

There is no reason why in this sense the most authentic form of assessment is that which most mimics industry, and using the earlier example a practical assessment, perhaps recorded, may prove to be the most effective measure of assessment. In many cases it may be best to employ the planning backwards method (McDonald 1992). In

Learning Outcome
2. Understand the impact of stress, arousal and anxiety on performance.
Grading Criteria

P4	P5	P6	M3	D2					
Bibliography (Y / N)				**Required**					

Scenario
You have been appointed by your local sports development department to work as a sport psychologist in preparing the local teams for their relevant competitions. You have been asked to prepare training materials for one of the sports of your choice.

Task 1

P4
P5
P6 Much research has been conducted into the positive and negative effects of stress, anxiety and arousal on sporting performance. Several theories have been developed and as such you are to prepare a presentation entitled:

"The causes of arousal, stress & anxiety in the sporting environment".

M3 Your presentation should fully outline why these factors occur during a sporting performance and the symptoms that are likely to be shown by the athlete. You must further explain the positive and negative effects of each of these. (M3).

D2 To achieve D2 you should further analyse the effects of arousal and outline the strengths and weaknesses of relevant arousal theory and come to a conclusion about the validity of each.

Further Guidance

· To describe the causes and effects of arousal you will need to define arousal and use a continuum to label different levels of arousal.

· To describe the relationship between arousal and performance you will have to cover a range of theories in a basic manner.

· To move from pass to merit you will have to provide more detail on the theories of the relationship between arousal and performance.

· To move from merit to distinction you will have to outline the strengths and weaknesses of each theory and come to a conclusion about the validity of each.

Figure 5.3 BTEC National Diploma – Sport and Exercise Science assignment

this approach the assessor decides on the desired outcome of the test and the learner is then encouraged to demonstrate their mastery of the problem set. The assessor makes their judgment based on an established set of competencies set in an authentic assessment environment. Although this may provide a greater sense of authenticity as in, say, work-based assessment of an NVQ, it does lead, as McDonald admits, to an assessment-led learning programme.

Practicability

Given the time available and the physical environment, is the assessment activity realistic? In some cases, it simply is not possible to arrange a totally authentic environment and we have to design a role play or case study, for example, as suggested in Chapter 4.

Differentiation

> Differentiation is . . . the process of identifying with each learner, the most effective strategies for achieving agreed targets.
>
> (Weston 1992)

> Differentiation is about identifying and addressing the different needs, interests and abilities of all learners to give them the best possible chance of achieving their learning goals.
>
> (DfES Standards Unit 2004)

In Chapter 4, we discussed the issues related to personalized learning and, as Brookfield (1998) observed, it can be very demanding if not impossible, to differentiate for every learner. However, we will no doubt be confronted with a class of individuals with different needs across the learning spectrum from very motivated and quick learners to those with special learning issues. As with all areas of teaching and learning, differentiation needs to be addressed within the assessment framework in order that each learner might be given every opportunity to demonstrate the quality of their learning. For example, all too often, assessments contain what are described as extension activities, which in reality are just activities that provide the more able with something to do, rather than something which challenges them and stretches their analytical, comparative or evaluative skills.

The key to a successfully differentiated assessment activity is in the planning stage, in other words, prior and recent knowledge of your learners, in order that you may design activities that promote access to all learners. Additional activities must be challenging and easily accessible. Increasingly it is necessary to establish personal targets and rely on good data from initial diagnostic assessment as well as reliable updates in documents such as Individual Learning Plans (ILPs) and learner passports to support assessment design.

Whatever the source, to ensure differentiation in sport and leisure assessment you must consider the following:

- practical ability
- maturity
- socio-economic status
- religious/cultural beliefs
- prior learning and knowledge including experience
- intrinsic motivation

- speed of learning
- specific individual need such as disability and language.

The assessor considering differentiated practice in assessment must also consider the use of peer and self-assessment, especially in mastery-type skills such as in discrete practical tasks.

The traditional 'Big Game' approach to the delivery of Physical Education is one which is slowly but steadily disappearing. The Big Game approach is centred on perhaps seven or eight individuals in a class of 30 learners who benefit from the process because of their ability, natural or learned, leaving the greater percentage of the group with no significant learning experience.

While there is inarguably a place for competitive sport, and by definition some will be better than others, it is necessary in the delivery and assessment of practical skills to explore the needs of the whole group, who are much better served in an ipsative fashion but practising in small groups or even alone a range of discrete skills where they can measure and record their own performance, such as for a skill circuit where personal bests are noted and targets are formally or informally set for improvement.

Reflection 5.6

To what extent has differentiation been embedded into the assignment in Figure 5.3?

How would you improve this aspect of planning in this example?

Assessment design

Many vocational sports programmes require the assessor to design the assessment material, and while this may be challenging, it should be considered an excellent opportunity to personalize assessment to suit a group of learners.

Consideration must be given to the following when planning assessment for a programme:

- the intended learning outcomes of the learning experience;
- the grading criteria assuming a criterion-based system;
- the most appropriate assessment tool (see next section);
- how feedback will be provided;
- how and when summative feedback is managed.

As we noted in Chapter 4, following the principles of constructive alignment (Biggs 2003), the starting point will almost certainly be the learning outcomes or criteria which define what it is the learner is expected to achieve. The assessment design, therefore, will reflect how we can best create opportunities for the learner to demonstrate their achievement of the outcomes.

Earlier, when considering coursework, we looked at a unit from a National Diploma programme (Figure 2.2): the learning outcomes are clearly identified, so this would be the guide to your setting assessment tasks. However, although the outcomes are generally explicit and relate to the acquisition of knowledge, understanding and skills, it is possible that they might reflect formative, process-based criteria such as in Reflection 5.7.

Reflection 5.7

The following is taken from an Edexcel specification for the National Diploma in Sport, Unit 30. *Impact and Sustainability in Outdoor Adventure*:

[The] grading criteria . . . require learners to plan, undertake and review a project based on the idea of environmental sustainability . . . It is a really good opportunity for learners to be autonomous and independent.

(Edexcel 2007: 287)

Could demonstrating 'autonomy and independence' in learning be considered an intended outcome? If so, how would you grade this?

From the learner's point of view, a clear assessment plan will enable them to engage more fully with the learning programme. In the spirit of autonomy, they will be able to organize their learning and integrate the assessment process into their own learning plan. It is also important to consider the impact of enabling learners' input in the design of their assessment and assisting them in recognizing their progress and achievement and developing a wider sense of responsibility for their own achievement in learning.

As previously mentioned, one of the challenges presented to new teachers on vocational programmes is the notion that they will be responsible for the design of assessment material. While this may at first appear to be daunting, when presented with a range of assessment tools and information about a group of learners, many report this as a key strength of vocational courses.

Whichever tool is chosen for assessment, we should ensure that we follow the principles of assessment discussed earlier, perhaps answering the following questions:

- Is the assessment a valid test of knowledge, understanding and skills? There should be no doubt what the assessment is measured against and, where possible, the criteria for assessment should be included. The task/s established to meet the criteria should be imaginative without ever deviating far from the assessment criteria.

- Is the assessment 'authentic'? Is it set in a realistic Sport and Leisure scenario which enables the learner to identify the purpose and context of the assessment? In a sense, this is a form of unsophisticated role play in which the learner may be asked to imagine a setting in which this assessment may be of value. A well-developed scenario can also influence career aims and extend an insight into a sport or perhaps fitness role that was not previously conceived.

- Does it differentiate appropriately? The assessment must be equitable and not exclude or disadvantage any member of any group to be assessed based on their gender, culture, disability, race or religious beliefs.

- Is it practicable? Assessment should be presented in such a way as to be easily accessed by the entire cohort. Increasingly there is a trend towards the use of technology in all aspects of teaching and learning. Assessment material previously presented in the form of a paper-based handbook may be more conveniently accessed electronically, for example, via a web portal or virtual learning network, and while this may suit the needs of most, there may well be some without regular internet access, and for whom the paper version remains the best option.

Assessment tools

Reflection 5.8

Think back over the last few courses that you have attended.

List at least ten different tests that you have done.

If you think that's too many, turn to Table 5.1 and see how many of your ideas are in that list.

Do you think that they were appropriate to what was being tested?

Table 5.1 List of possible forms of assessment

Written	Media-based	Practical
Poster presentation/ Leaflet presentation	Audio or video recording	Survey
Product evidence/artefact	Website design	Project
Practical sport/exercise logbook	Podcast	Field-based experiment
Presentation	Post to forum (text, audio or video)	Role play
Work-based assessment	Recorded discussion	Performance observation case studies
Portfolio of evidence	Annotated photographs	Witness statements or Observation records
Reflective journal	Recorded audio submission	Peer assessment
		Practical assignment
		Simulation
		Sports coaching or leadership performance

Selection of the right kind of assessment is of significant importance when you consider the process of centre-based assessment design. It must fulfil the criteria that we have looked at earlier.

In addition to the criteria for assessment, the very essence of vocational learning is in the development of a range of skills that will prove useful in the workplace, in this case the sport or active leisure workplace. So the format must have wide-ranging potential and be vocationally relevant, stimulating and challenging.

Awarding bodies generally suggest a range of assessment tools, but almost always point to those designing assessments to be innovative, creative, and design assessment to fit their own local needs.

Reflection 5.9

Having reflected on the list of possible assessment 'tools' in Table 5.1 and perhaps added some of your own, now turn to the list of programme outcomes in Figure 5.4 and try to decide what you think would be the most appropriate assessment tool for each one.

Remember to apply the principles of validity, reliability and authenticity to your choice.

- Understand the respiratory system and how it is affected by exercise (level 2)
- Plan and lead Adventurous Outdoor Activities (level 3)
- Assess own performance in selected team sports (level 3)
- Understand the key concepts of sports development particularly barriers to participation (level 3)
- Undertake a risk assessment before leading an activity session (level 2)
- Know about the provision of exercise for specific groups such as the disabled, pre-natal, older adults and children (level 3)
- Understand why people take part in sport (level 2)
- Know the psychological factors which influence sport performance (level 2)
- Prepare and use equipment for a multi-day expedition (level 3)
- Understand what makes a successful sports business (level 3)
- Know how exercise affects the anaerobic and aerobic energy systems (level 2)
- Be able to undertake an environmentally sustainable project (level 3: Outdoor Adventurous Activity)

Figure 5.4 Assessment criteria

Assessment for learning

Although, for the most part we have tried to address the issues of assessment *of* learning, which tends to be *summative*, we did briefly touch on formative assessment or assessment *for* learning, in our introduction to this chapter. That this is an essential element of the learning process is, generally, undisputed. Black and Wiliam in their small but much quoted booklet, *Inside the Black Box* suggest that this means, 'An assessment activity [that] can help learning if it provides information to be used as feedback, by teachers and their pupils, to modify the teaching and learning activities in which they are engaged' (1998: 5).

Giving feedback

Earlier, we also observed how feedback is, of course, essential to the process of learning, whether it is internalized by the learner analysing their own performance, or if it comes externally such as by a peer or a teacher. By assessing the actual outcomes of our efforts and matching them to the intended outcomes, we can, if necessary, modify our behaviour or work to meet with success. So it is most important that we include space for feedback at several intervals in our assessment plan and, again, this should be included in our scheme of work.

There is little that can be more demotivating to a learner than negative feedback: that is, feedback that only focuses on the faults, for we can learn as much from our successes as from our faults, and possibly more. So, feedback should be supportive and adapted to the specific learner's needs, guiding them to recognize what they have achieved and encouraging them to extend themselves more. It could also include an opportunity for the learner to have an input, through questioning, so they develop a critical stance to their own work and, incidentally, hone their skills of autonomous learning.

Reflection 5.10

In Chapter 2, we asked you to mark a piece of work from a student who had written quite competently about fitness testing, but who needed help with their literacy skills (Box 3.1).

With the benefit of what you have now read, write some feedback which is at once encouraging yet also developmental. This means that it should read a little more positively than, 'Good content: poor use of language'!

Verification and moderation: quality management

Finally, we should ask the question, 'How do I know that my assessment plan or assignment is acceptable to the awarding body, the institution and, of course, the learners?'

The learners will let you know soon enough if they cannot understand the assignment, or if they think that it doesn't reflect the intended learning outcomes, but what of the other stakeholders? If this is your first attempt at designing assessment, there should be help at hand through a process of internal and external verification and moderation. Although the two may sometimes be confused and the distinction between them blurred, essentially verification implies a bureaucratic authentication or rubber stamping, whereas moderation suggests a less formal process of comparison and standardization of grading: a discussion between assessors and an experienced, appointed Moderator.

Although different centres may have different quality management systems, there will generally be a fully qualified Internal Verifier whose role it is to critically examine all assessments before they are presented to learners. They will, of course, check that it fulfils all the criteria for the proposed unit of assessment and also that it conforms to the principles of assessment that we have discussed at some length. This Verifier should be prepared to advise you even before you embark on the process of design.

When the assessment has been graded and moderated by the programme team through a process of cross-grading and discussion, the Internal Verifier will sample a cross-section of assessments and agree to appropriate standards.

The whole process is monitored carefully by the Awarding Bodies through a system of External Moderators who do the same job as the Internal Verifier, checking assessment briefs and standardizing grading but, of course, with reference to a wide range of other centres, thus ensuring reliability in the assessment practices of each centre. It is their role to judge the efficacy of the internal verification systems and in this respect their role is a critical one: if there are major discrepancies in the verification and moderation systems, they have the power to block a centre's authority to grant certification to learners completing their programmes.

Summary

A central theme to this chapter has been to try to view assessment as an essential element in the process of learning. It is our way of finding out, in the first instance, what our learners bring to the learning environment (diagnostic assessment), and then what they learn either as they progress through the programme of learning (formative assessment) or at the end (summative assessment). Essentially it is about judging 'the quality of student achievement' (Armitage and Renwick 2007: 5).

The role of feedback is seen as central to this learning process, whether it is based on our own self-assessment or that of another person, a peer or a teacher: how else can we know about the quality of our learning? So we have considered how this feedback can best be supportive of learning and have decided that it must first focus on the positive elements of the outcomes of the assessment before addressing any areas for improvement.

However, it is just as important that the assessment activities by which we make these judgements are equal to the task of measuring what it is that we hope the students have learnt. We have, therefore, looked at the principles that underpin assessment design and at the methods and tools currently at our disposal.

Assessment design should be seen to be relevant to the learners' needs and to the content and context of the programme. It should, in other words, be a valid assessment reflecting the realities of their programmes in the wider world of Sport and Leisure, whether that be in an occupational role, such as for an NVQ, or in higher education as an academic field of study. It should be a means by which our learners can demonstrate the quality of their learning, not an instrument designed to find out their deficiencies.

Finally, we have tried to contextualize assessment within the various programmes on which our learners will have enrolled and have noted the differences in the ways that they are assessed. On the one hand, NVQs will assess practical skills, although, as we have seen, even they have an element of knowledge and understanding: it is not enough to be able to 'plan a coaching session', coaches need to be able to articulate the reasons for good planning and to identify and understand the needs of the participants. On the other hand, A level Sport Studies will demand in-depth study of a variety of academic aspects of sport such as anatomy and physiology, biomechanics, psychology, sociology and historical development, and this might best be tested through examinations. Then again, we have programmes, such as National Diplomas, assessed by continuous coursework requiring the learner to develop skills of research and analysis in order to learn the subject content independently.

We hope that this will have helped you to have developed not only a range of strategies for assessment but also a rationale for your choice. Perhaps, too, it will have motivated you to find ways of creating models that will make the process of assessment a more enjoyable, stimulating and challenging experience for your learners.

6

Maximizing the use of resources

In this chapter we will be looking at:

- How resources can support learning and teaching in the Sport and Leisure curriculum
- Identifying and preparing resources appropriate to the needs of their learners
- The teacher as resource
- Developing resources to support classroom teaching
- Resources that enhance autonomous learning, such as textbooks and internet access
- Resourcing learning and teaching in the varied learning environments of the Sport and Leisure sector
- Making links and partnerships with Sport and Leisure organizations and practitioners to enhance the learning experience, including educational visits
- Making the most of the work placement as a resource

Using resources to support learning and teaching in the Sport and Leisure curriculum

Well-prepared and appropriate resources are an important aid to support, motivate and reinforce learning in any subject, and this is certainly true of the Sport and Leisure curriculum. We saw in Chapter 1 how our learners are generally active participants and this means that, in a classroom environment, it is particularly important that they are engaged in active learning which, in turn, will most likely involve the use of stimulating resources. On the other hand, many of our teaching and learning activities will be of a practical nature which will involve management of specialist environments to maximize their potential as learning resources.

For our purposes, we have found it convenient to consider resources for Sport and Leisure under these two categories: (1) the classroom in which we generally address theoretical topics; and (2) the wider environments where we engage in experiential learning, the practical application of theory and applied learning. The latter would include environments such as the fitness gym, the sports centre, the swimming pool, the playing field and the Great Outdoors. However, this is not to say that these should be considered as separate, unrelated environments: the one complements the other. Practical activities should be informed by theory, and practical activity is the way in which we test the validity of the theory. So we need to ensure that resources for practical activities are adequate to support the application of theory.

In the classroom, we shall consider first how resources can support the teacher in preparing meaningful learning experiences, and then how we deploy these resources to develop our students as autonomous learners. We will see how modern electronic technology has changed our classrooms, but will also acknowledge the use of non-electronic resources, such as textbooks, journals, hard-copy handouts and pen boards.

The wider Sport and Leisure environments are too vast to consider each separately within this publication, so our focus will be more generally on how to make the most of them in terms of experiential learning, which we discussed in Chapter 4.

Finally, as we also briefly mentioned in Chapter 4, nowhere provides a more realistic environment better than the workplace, so we will address the planning of educational visits and work placements as an essential resource for the teacher of Sport and Leisure. We might add here the value of inviting speakers to share their current experiences in the industry with your classes.

As we saw in Chapter 2, the programme specifications, the scheme of work and the lesson plan are your starting point for planning. Here we explore resources that assist in taking the learning objectives off the page to become a learning experience.

Resources that enhance learning and teaching in the classroom

The teacher as a resource

There is probably no more important resource in any of the learning environments discussed so far than you, as the teacher. The effectiveness of the programme effectively revolves around your own wealth of expertise and knowledge. As a teacher of Sport and Leisure, you are expected to maintain an in-depth knowledge of the subject, just as in any other subject.

Reflection 6.1

Thinking about the breadth of your own experiences in Sport and Leisure as a client, employee or student, take a few moments to consider what you can offer to your students to enhance their knowledge and understanding of the industry.

However, even knowing that we are the experts in our subject, there are few other subjects that feature so largely in the public domain as Sport and Leisure, as we saw in Chapter 1. Nearly everyone enrolled on your programmes, of whatever age, will have a view informed at least by the media and, possibly, in-depth experience of active participation. The answer to this challenge is to ensure that when you enter a classroom, you are fully prepared. Your subject knowledge must be of sufficient depth to ensure that you can use the teaching skills you are developing to make each lesson a valuable learning experience. This chapter will assist in ensuring that your knowledge is up to date and accurate. Remember that when you say something as a teacher, there is an expectation (quite rightly) that you know what you are talking about.

Reflection 6.2

Thinking about some of the issues discussed in Chapter 1, what do you think are the most recent developments in the Sport and Leisure Industry?

How confident are you that your subject knowledge is up to date?

How could you update your knowledge and understanding of current policies and practices in the industry?

You may have a degree in the subject and/or some experience from working in the industry. This helps you understand topic areas of the Sport and Leisure subject syllabus, but don't fall into the trap of planning all your lessons only around the areas you know, your role is to bring the whole syllabus (and industry if appropriate) to the learning experience. Your own learning must continue for you to do this. Sources of information are vast, including textbooks, television, the internet, DVDs, industry organizations, work shadowing and visiting speakers, so be prepared to engage with them all in the process of your own professional development. If you work in the life-long learning sector, you will know that this is now a part of your contract, a requirement of your membership of the Institute for Learning (IfL), and in schools too you will be expected to undertake such continuing professional development.

The learners

While the teacher and visiting speakers might have a wider experience of the Sport and Leisure industry, we should also value the experiences that our learners bring to the programme. As we have seen, all will have some experience of PE at school and it is hard to ignore the influence of the media, but many will also have belonged to sports clubs. Indeed, you may find that some have experience of performing at a very high level. The expert teacher will be able to draw on these experiences to enhance the learning of the whole group.

Reflection 6.3

Jason belonged to the local swimming club, was a County champion and was on the verge of being selected for the national squad. He trained for two hours most mornings before attending college and also most evenings. At college, he was studying for a BTEC National in Sport Science.

What aspects of his participation in sport might a teacher be able to draw upon to enhance the learning experience of the whole group?

How could the teacher integrate this into the learning programme?

Reflection 6.4

Claire has a daytime job as a financial consultant, but has been attending Yoga classes for some years now and is hoping to qualify as a teacher of Yoga in the near future.

She is currently attending your level 2 (OCN) Anatomy and Physiology class.

What special knowledge and understanding might she be able to contribute to the class?

How might you try to integrate this into your lessons?

Resources that support teaching and learning

We have frequently made reference to the fact that, if our teaching is to be meaningful for our learners, then we should be creating interactive learning environments that stimulate and engage them, and the way that we use resources to support our lessons has an important role to play in this process. Here we shall first consider resources based on electronic technology and then non-electronic resources.

Resources based on electronic technology

The pace of technological change has seen a rapid growth in the development of electronic resources that can give us easy and instant access to information and support tools that can make our teaching more stimulating for our learners, particularly the younger adults for many of whom such technology is an accepted part of their everyday life. As teachers we should not be fearful of these developments but should embrace them, and use our learners' knowledge and understanding of them to our advantage. On the other hand, we should also be aware that not all learners have such ready access to this technology when away from the institution and that they could be at a disadvantage were we to assume that they can work independently at home. Also, as we saw in Chapter 3, some may be fearful of modern technology and might need considerable support to develop even basic skills, particularly more mature adults.

However, it is fast becoming the norm to use technological resources such as PowerPoint in the classroom to support the teacher's presentation, so we will now consider how to make the best use of some of these, with the proviso that, by the time of publication, the likelihood is that we may well already be out of date!

Using PowerPoint presentations

Reflection 6.5

What are the key features of the slide shown in Figure 6.1?

What are its main flaws (if there are any)?

Would you have designed this differently?

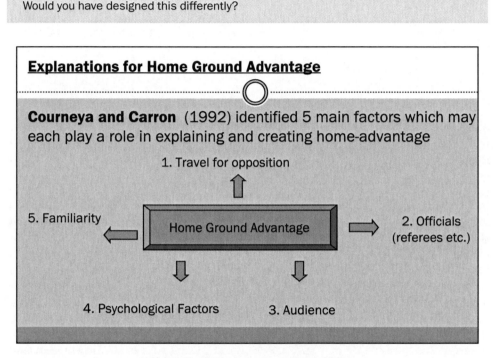

Figure 6.1 Exemplar PowerPoint slide

The importance and strength of a PowerPoint presentation (or in the Apple Mac version, Keynote) are that it will help to reinforce learning by providing a visual stimulus. Whether we accept the principle of learning styles, that we are fulfilling the needs of the visual learner, or are, like Coffield et al. (2004), more sceptical (see Chapter 4), the visual impact of the PowerPoint does underpin and provide a focus to our delivery. It will identify key words and ideas that the learner can note down and, used creatively with illustrations, can be a potent aid to learning. Figure 6.1 is an example of such a slide.

Reflection 6.6

You may remember the most ineffective PowerPoint presentation that you've suffered – even if you can't remember what it was about, often they are the most memorable.

Why was it a poor example of this medium?

Which features needed to be improved?

Furthermore, the potential of PowerPoint can be considerably enhanced by the introduction of hyperlinks. These links will enable you and the learner to access websites and video clips for supplementary information at the click of a mouse! It is not within the scope of this publication to instruct the reader in these processes, but programs, such as PowerPoint, have inbuilt instructions that are easy to follow. Figure 6.2 is an example of a slide with a hyperlink inserted: by clicking on 'insert' in the taskbar and then 'hyperlink', you can easily insert a link to internet websites. When you show the presentation to a class, you can click on the link and instantly refer to its contents.

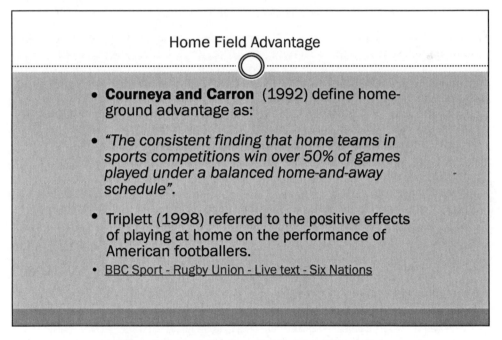

Figure 6.2 Exemplar PowerPoint slide with hyperlink

Problems with PowerPoint

PowerPoint can be a very potent tool, but it is not without its pitfalls. The 'death by PowerPoint' syndrome is well known in education and training circles. Presentations of 40 or 50 slides are not unknown, and this can be counter-productive. Instead of stimulating the learner, this is more likely to send them to sleep! It would suggest that the presenter is relying on the slides for the content of the session and possibly merely reading from them rather than using them as a stimulus. This is hardly interactive teaching and learning: the PowerPoint should be used to support learning, not replace it.

The slide in our example gives important, yet minimal information which is helpfully bullet-pointed, leaving the teacher and the learner to fill in the gaps through question and answer and discussion. In an overcrowded slide, the important points can easily be lost. Furthermore, your slides will be much more memorable and interesting if they are illustrated by importing pictures from Clip-Art or perhaps photographs.

Important guidelines then would be:

- Do not use too many slides.
- Do not overcrowd any slide with information.
- Make the slides memorable where possible by using illustrations.
- Insert hyperlinks to make a wider range of information accessible.

Making your presentations accessible to your learners

There is·a tendency for audiences at a presentation, whether in your class or at a conference, to want to write down everything they see on the slides. However, this is unnecessary and distracting for them, and can be pre-empted by copying the presentation onto an internal website such as Blackboard or Moodle and making this available to your learners, perhaps with the warning that downloading the presentation is no substitute for attending your lessons!

Of course, it is also possible to print off hard copies with space for making notes as in our example Figure 6.3, opposite. This has the advantage that, should the technology fail or not be available, you will still be able to use the presentation albeit in a much more limited fashion. The problem here is to know when to give out the hard-copy handouts. You want the learners to have them available to make notes that complement the presentation, yet if you give them out too early, they will perhaps read ahead of your input and not focus on the discussion in hand. One way of dealing with this is to give out the pages of the handout in stages rather than all at once at the beginning.

Interactive White Boards (IWBs)

An interactive white board is essentially a multi-layered surface which will accept the display of a projector or camera. It is activated either by touch of hand or a stylus. It will give you, the tutor and learners the ability to draw, write and create unique documents, and save them as part of a recognizable text document for whatever reason (see Figure 6.4).

Consider the advantage to the sport learner who can import sporting performances, leadership video clips or even fitness assessments directly from video devices. Because everything created can be saved, it means that whole lessons can be captured and retrieved at any point, potentially particularly useful for absentees or for revision.

IWBs can deliver contemporary, exciting interactivities across an expanding range of subject areas such as for anatomy or fitness training principles.

2/13/2010

Narcotic Analgesics
Names – codeine, morphine, heroin

Reason – to evade pain of injury or used to mask
injury.

Side effects – addiction, state of stupor.

Sports associated – all sports.

_____
_____
_____
_____
_____
_____
_____

Beta Blockers
Name – Atntolol, Metapolol

Reason – slows heart rate, steadies nerves, feeling of
Calm.

Side effects – reduces circulation, causes fatigue
and shortness of breath

Sports associated – snooker, darts, shooting.

_____
_____
_____
_____
_____
_____
_____

Diuretics
Names – Frupil and Bunnex

Reason – quick loss of weight, removes other drugs
from system quickly.

Side effects – dehydration, cramps, overheating,
irregular heartbeat.

Sports associated – horse racing, boxing, rowing.

_____
_____
_____
_____
_____
_____
_____

Figure 6.3 Exemplar PowerPoint note-taking page

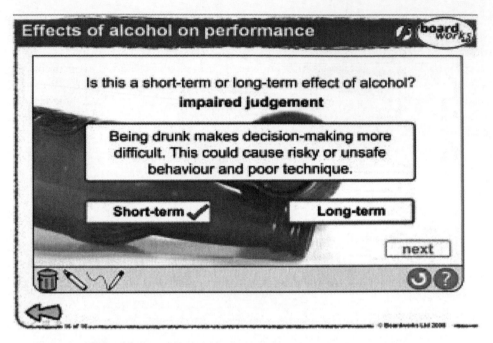

Figure 6.4 Print-out of an interactive white board presentation

The use of these boards is now widespread and expanding, and it is claimed that their use enables learners to understand new concepts and allows the tutor to plan and to engage all learners.

Video, DVD and CD-Rom – specialized sports analysis software

The filming and projection of moving images provide an invaluable resource in bringing Sport and Leisure to life in the classroom and there are a number of applications we can use.

Reflection 6.7

Try to recall all the different ways that you have used moving images to enhance learning or to supplement your own attempts at describing some difficult concept.

Using online video clips

High quality broadband provision, streaming technology and the ability to rip or download video clips have made a significant impact on all areas of learning, not least that of Sport and Leisure.

The ease of personal video uploading to sites like Google video, YouTube and Facebook is unquestionable, but these sites are not without their detractors with fears about content and the need to ensure safeguarding of vulnerable learners at the core of these concerns.

It cannot be denied, however, that the appropriate and responsible use of these sites has a great deal of potential for the Sport and Leisure learner. Access to up-to-the-minute clips can enhance any lecture and emphasize points with clarity.

Video sharing capabilities are endless, but consider the merits of uploading a practical sporting performance for assessment. Consider also the ability to give feedback as an assessor using the same approach. Video uploads by a whole class or sub-unit could be uploaded to such a site and linked to the secure VLE for assessment and comment.

Video clips of sports men and women might be used to illustrate particular aspects of a topic, such as the acquisition of skill, for example. Recordings of team games might provide opportunities to analyse strategy. Also, there are a number of commercially produced packages illustrating body functions such as the circulatory system, all of which can help you in your explanations of what otherwise can seem to be rather mysterious to the learner and can be difficult to describe. Companies such as SSER Ltd and Online Classroom.tv have extensive catalogues from which to choose.

In fact, there are so many versions of these packages in the market that the choice can be daunting. Base level analysis tools will allow the import of digital video clips and allow analysis of that clip via a network licence. Figure 6.5, overleaf, gives a diagrammatic example of some of the applications of this kind of software.

However, as always, there is a note of caution: the video is not a substitute for your teaching. It should be used to enhance learning and should be accompanied by preparation and debrief as always in order to contextualize the topic. While watching yet another episode of *Fawlty Towers* may be engaging, funny and entertaining for your class, it has no real significance unless discussed in the context of customer service or even of management skills.

Video cameras and mobile phones

Cameras of a very reasonable quality are relatively cheap now and are easy to use. Many of your learners will be quite expert in their use and you may find that their mobile phones have this facility. Since younger adults, at least, appear to be addicted to the 'mobile', why not put them to constructive use?

Creating our own videos can be a most useful tool, especially to enhance our Sport and Leisure programmes. Perhaps the most important use is to record performance, either a sporting performance or perhaps a role play or group presentation. This can then be played back for analysis or even for assessment. Indeed, creating a video might even be the assessment method.

Reflection 6.8

How many ways might you have used video to assess performance in a Sport and Leisure programme?

How could you use a learner-produced video as an alternative means of assessment for an assignment?

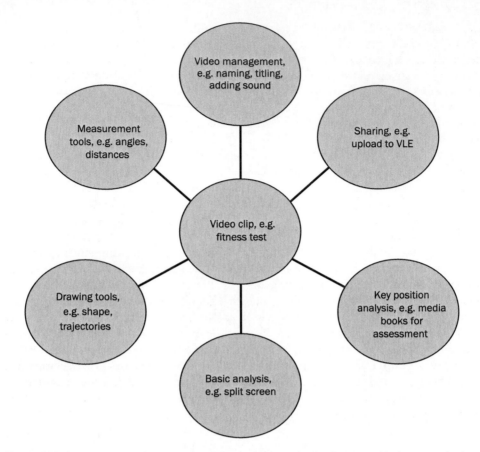

Figure 6.5 Suggested application of software packages in the Sport and Leisure curriculum

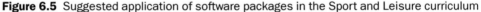

Other, non-electronic resources

Unfortunately, the technology is not necessarily always as reliable or available as we might like it to be, so it is always important to have an alternative resource at hand and to have the skills to use it.

White boards

Where interactive boards are not available, generally there will be a white board on which you can write with the appropriate marker pens. Again, this is still an important resource to promote interactive learning. It allows you to write up learner responses to questions, thus showing that you value their contribution. It allows you to respond in the moment to the development of the lesson, perhaps developing a model to structure information, as already suggested, in the form of a flow-chart. It allows you to write up key words that your learners will need to know for that lesson and to note lesson objectives that they can check during the session.

Flip-charts

Board work can often be complemented or even substituted by the use of a flip-chart. It can be useful to record information (such as key words or lesson objectives) that you want to retain throughout the session and that might otherwise be rubbed off the board.

However, the flip-chart is a flexible resource that has another important role in the interactive lesson. It can be used so that the learners can, generally in group work, create posters to display their responses to discussions as a focus to presentations. These can then be displayed on the classroom walls as a reminder of the outcomes of their work.

Handouts

We have already referred to handouts as a way of distributing our PowerPoint presentations to learners. However, they clearly have a wider use. They can provide supplementary information gleaned from a variety of sources such as articles photocopied from journals, photographs of sportsmen and women in action and summaries of important aspects of a lesson. As with the PowerPoint presentation, overload should be avoided: learners are far more likely to read something that is relatively uncluttered and if there is not too much paper involved.

They will be of much greater value if they are used as a stimulus to learning and are accompanied by questions perhaps to ensure that the learners do actually refer to them.

A development of the handout is the 'gapped handout' in which key words are left out for the learner to complete. This can be particularly useful to make notes from a presentation where the teacher has provided a certain amount of information but has left out phrases or words, the answer to which will be found during the presentation.

Resources that enhance autonomous learning

So far we have considered resources that enable the teacher to develop an interactive environment with their learners. However, for the learner to take greater responsibility for their own learning, they need to be able to access sources of information that will develop their knowledge and understanding and also to have the means to produce a record of their findings. Clearly, electronic sources will feature highly in this, but so will paper sources such as books, journals and magazines.

Textbooks

Publications that will support the development of the learner range from workbooks for GCSE learners to engage in question and answer exercises, such as those produced by SSER (see Figure 6.6), to textbooks that are written with a particular programme in mind, such as the A levels or National Diplomas, with exercises and activities to encourage learners to reflect and research.

While these publications are invaluable sources of information and can help the teacher with their planning, there is a danger that the learner will become too reliant

What is Recovery?

One of the key benefits of regular exercise is faster recovery.

Recovery is the process of the body returning to the _____ state once exercise has stopped. The recovery time depends upon the _____ of exercise and the _____ of the person.

There are four key parts to the recovery process. List them below:

1)   _____ rate
2)   _____ _____ removal
3)   _____ stores
4)   _____ repair

Recovery and the Heart

During recovery, the heart rate should steadily return to its normal _____ heart rate.

For the same exercise, the _____ you are, the _____ the recovery.

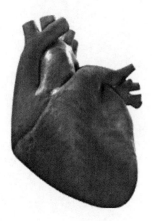

For a Fit Person

The heart of a fit person recovers much _____ – it slows down much _____ once exercising stops.

For an Unfit Person

The heart of an unfit person recovers much _____ – it takes _____ to slow down once exercising stops.

Figure 6.6 Extract from Workbook by SSER: Exercise Recovery

on them. The danger is that they will look no further and that this will result in the 'surface learning' that we discussed in Chapter 4. They will consider that the 'answers' that they need to pass the assignment are all in the book and will reproduce the information just as set out therein. The teacher is then left with the daunting task of marking large numbers of assignments that all appear to be the same and with no real originality. Clearly, the way in which assignments are written, as discussed in Chapter 5, must ensure that the learner is encouraged to reflect on experience and research more widely.

Internet access

There are two important ways in which you can use internet resources as a teacher. First, you can use them to support your own work in preparing your programmes and lessons, and, second, their use can be embedded into your programmes to enhance learning and to enable your learners to research sources for information.

Supporting teaching through the internet

In the first instance, there are a number of websites designed by teachers for teachers and dedicated to sharing information about educational resources, within which you will be able to access subject-specific information. These are generally called 'gateway' sites since they provide you with routes to other useful resources. Specially recommended by Geoff Petty (2009: 405) are the following:

> http://excellence.qia.org.uk/
> www.intute.ac.uk/
> www.bbc.co.uk/learning/
> www.curriculumonline.gov.uk/

We would add:

> http://www.bized.co.uk/
> http://teachers.net/
> http://www.lsnlearning.org.uk/

Finally, but not exhaustively, the site provided by The Higher Education Academy, Hospitality, Leisure, Sport and Tourism Network which aims to encourage and broker the sharing of good learning and teaching practice:

> http://www.heacademy.ac.uk/hlst/ourwork/heinfe/teachingexchange.

Supporting learning through the internet

The second way that we can use the internet is to embed its use into our schemes of work and lesson plans (see Chapters 2, 3 and 4), thus encouraging our learners to use it constructively to develop their knowledge and understanding while also developing their key and functional skills.

There are also, of course, problems with managing the 'virtual learning environment'. Our younger students in particular will be familiar with ICT and many use it for playing games and communication. Constant vigilance is required to ensure that they remain 'on task' and that they are not distracted by attractive alternatives.

The amount of information available through the internet is vast and it is an invaluable tool to enhance your students' learning. The problem is being able to refine the research. Of course, your learners can use a search engine but typing in 'National Parks' on Google, for example, will give you 160 million entries. Of course, refining this to the UK will reduce the entries considerably but there are still far too many to process easily, so it is useful to build up a data base of websites of your own or access a 'gateway' site that has already done the job for you: one such website dedicated to providing information about other related websites is www.britishsports.com.

Virtual Learning Environments (VLEs)

As technology reshapes forever the way in which education is delivered, assessed and even managed, the evolution of the Virtual Learning Environment is perhaps the most significant innovation in recent times.

For more than ten years educationalists have explored the notion of a web-based platform that could allow the storage for easy access of a range of teaching and learning materials, perhaps the most important role of the VLE thus far.

Effectively a software package that allows the assessor, by remote access, the ability to access tools such as assessment graders, test setting software, electronic assessment or return of student work, the VLE or perhaps less formally a basis of inexpensive electronic communication via forums is invaluable.

In addition to this, the VLE also allows the learner the ability to access lecture notes, assessment activities, peer communication and even the submission of course-work, critically by remote and secure access.

From an organizational point of view, it is fast becoming a tool for learner survey, a data bank of a variety of useful institutional data about remote access and interactivity. Plagiarism is easier to detect in conjunction with the correct software, e.g. Turnitin.

Many centres have now subscribed to VLEs such as Fronter and Moodle, which boast a range of possibilities such as initial diagnostic assessment, or perhaps more excitingly the unprecedented opportunity for the sharing of resources across sector education areas.

Resources in applied learning environments

As we have already noted, environments in which Sport and Leisure takes place are wide and varied. We will try to see how we can maximize their potentials in enhancing the curriculum. Apart from providing the environment in which we can participate in our chosen activities, how can we use them for learning? The focus here should be on putting skills, knowledge and understanding into practice. This could be practical performance skills, as for the practical GCSE/A levels or ND Sports Performance, or occupational skills as for managing groups on the CSLA programme or coaching, teaching and instructing, maintenance of facilities and fitness testing.

As with all our learning environments, preparation is an imperative and, in the case of Sport and Leisure which almost by definition includes an element of risk, we must pay special attention to issues of Health and Safety. These are generally obvious, but guidelines will be laid down by your institution and by the various stakeholders with an interest and we do deal with this later in more detail. But basically, we should ensure that the activity surfaces are appropriate (clean floors/level playing areas, for example) and that equipment is in good condition and safe (no loose components on fixed weights apparatus, for example).

However, having made sure that the environment is safe, how do we maximize its potential as a learning resource? Of course, this may depend on the equipment that is available: you may be able to carry out fitness tests in a dedicated laboratory, for example, or a fitness circuit in a gym, but you may also have to adapt to carrying out tests in a classroom environment with minimal equipment. Making sure that you have the equipment or can book the laboratory will more than justify the preparation through the scheme of work discussed in Chapter 2.

Although it may be nice to think that you can run a netball coaching course with one ball between two participants, how would you plan to keep 20 people occupied and make the most of the learning situation if you only have four netballs?

Reflection 6.9

Consider the Sport and Leisure learning environments listed below and bearing in mind the discussion above, what planning would you undertake to prepare for the session?

1   Leading a one day map-reading expedition in wild country.
2   Carrying out a diagnostic test for a client starting a fitness programme.
3   Taking a group working towards a level 2 netball coaching award.

What would be your minimum requirements to ensure that this was a successful experience?

Using people as a resource

Visiting speakers

Visiting speakers who are currently working in the Sport and Leisure environment will help to contextualize your learners' studies. There are many organizations such as the local authority sports development department, private health clubs or Adventurous Activity Centres that are happy either to provide speakers or to offer visits. As we observed in Chapter 4, the trick here is that your preparation provides an experience to meet learning outcomes. The preparation should begin by ensuring that the timing of a talk from an 'industry expert' is complementary to your scheme of work. It is also necessary to ensure that the speaker is aware of your planned learning outcomes and how their contribution fits with these outcomes. A speaker for a speaker's sake will lose your credibility with your learning group very quickly, particularly with older groups of learners.

As a safety check, you should ensure the speaker is comfortable talking to large groups and knows to whom they will be speaking, their audience. People not familiar with teaching may need guidance. For example, if it is a young group, the speaker may need to adjust their use of language to an appropriate level, so that it is neither too complicated nor too simple. If jargon is going to be used, it should be explained: people who work with jargon tend to forget the rest of the world does not understand it. It is helpful to display key words on a board or chart. You should perhaps advise the speaker to consider carefully if what they are going to say, will be acceptable or perhaps be found funny or embarrassing by a group of teenagers? The presentation needs to be in a logical order that will not confuse the learners; the speaker may require some of your expert help in preparing the talk to ensure clarity of message.

Most importantly, you will need to confirm that the speaker provides the outcomes the learners require from the talk; an interesting talk does not always translate into a report on Customer Service, which the group have to produce for the assessment. Time spent preparing the speaker will overcome issues later.

Preparation of the learners will further maximize the learning outcomes from the occasion. If the talk is carefully planned into your scheme of work, the relevance and context will be apparent to the learners. However, you can enhance the learning by preparing resources, such as a gapped handout with headings under which topics discussed can be captured, and which may be completed immediately after the talk. Be careful of expecting the learners to remember what the speaker said in the lesson a week previously.

Preparation using syllabus or assessment criteria or with the learners' contributions to understanding the learning process

Preparing pupils through an exercise where they generate their own questions to which they require answers from the syllabus or assessment criteria may help their development as autonomous learners by:

1　Focusing on the outcome needed for learning or assessment.
2　Developing the learners' own planning and learning skills.

Having secured your speaker, it is important to make the experience enjoyable for them too so they will support you in future. Your learners need to show respect for the speaker who has given up their time to address them and, importantly, interact with them in an intelligent manner. Visitors coming in from outside of the educational environment wish to feel valued: silence by a group may be seen as a lack of valuing the experience. Thus it is important during the planning process to ensure that the learners prepare their questions to maximize the benefits gained from the occasion.

Reflection 6.10

You have booked the manager of the local council-run leisure centre to give a presentation on customer service to your Advanced Diploma group of mainly 16–17-year-olds.

What measures would you take to prepare the speaker:

1   To cover the learning outcomes?
2   To help them relate to the group?

Finally, you need to ensure that all technology is working before commencement of the talk: it can be very embarrassing for a speaker whose presentation is focused on PowerPoint slides to find that the projector is not working.

Remember you must ask permission from the appropriate authorities to bring a visitor into a school or college, and that the person should be Criminal Record Bureau (CRB) checked if they are to be left alone with your class.

External organizations

Again, in Chapter 4, we considered the importance of practical experience in the occupational environment. In this respect, making links with employers, although time-consuming, is a valuable exercise and offers great rewards.

Establishing good relationships with managers of local leisure centres or of private sports and health clubs can open all kinds of opportunities. We have seen how they may be willing to give presentations to your learners but, better still, they may be prepared to show you round their facility and give a talk on site. Furthermore, you may be able to make an arrangement for your groups to use the facilities either informally or as a part of the programme and, of course, they may provide another outlet for work-based learning.

Teaching outside of the classroom

Much of your practical work will take place outside of the classroom or even off the premises and in outdoor adventurous environments in which challenge is implicit. This might be on a regular basis for activities or for specially organized educational trips either for a day or perhaps over an extended period of time.

We have already noted how Sport and Leisure activities are inherently dangerous, and this is, at least partially, their appeal. So, in terms of your responsibilities, there are two seemingly conflicting aspects that you should consider. On the one hand, the Royal Society for the Prevention of Accidents (ROSPA) advises, 'Teachers are obliged to take all reasonable measures to ensure that every child under their control and supervision is safe and protected from any unacceptable risks. The teacher must be CAREFUL not CARELESS. Being careless is, in legal terms, being negligent; and being negligent means that you might be liable' (ROSPA 2001).

On the other hand, however, the DfES advised that, 'The school curriculum should ... enable pupils to respond positively to opportunities, challenges and responsibilities, to manage risk and to cope with change and adversity' (DfES and QCA 1999: 3). The dilemma for the teacher of Sport and Leisure, then, is how to maintain the balance for our learners by ensuring that, while providing every opportunity for them to experience the occupational environment in the widest possible contexts, they also take every precaution to minimize the risks.

Clearly some environments involve more risks than others. At the extreme end of a continuum from low risk to high, we should be aware of the inherent risks in Sport and Leisure involving adventurous outdoor activities such as skiing or canoeing. ROSPA gives the following examples of potential dangers and the outcomes:

- Four children lost their lives when they were swept out to sea off the rocks at Land's End; four boys died when they slid over a precipice in Austria.
- Four sixth formers died in a canoeing accident at Lyme Bay in Dorset.
- Twelve children and a teacher died when their minibus crashed into the back of a maintenance vehicle on the hard shoulder of the M40.

As a result of any tragic incident involving school children, questions are asked, procedures are tightened, and new legislation may come into force. A case in point is the *Activity Centres (Young Person's Safety) Act* 1995 and the *Adventure Activities Licensing Regulations* 1996 which resulted from the Lyme Bay incident. The ROSPA website provides excellent advice for making such field trips safer.

Nobody would suggest that these are common accidents but, by definition, they are unexpected and probably arising from apparently innocuous situations. The teacher needs to be constantly aware of the dangers.

Planning the educational field visit

Before planning a visit, for groups of all ages whether young or more mature adults, there must be effective planning for this teaching strategy just as there is in classroom-based methods.

First, we need to make sure that the visit is meaningful and will enhance learning for our groups. It is worth repeating that it should provide an opportunity to contextualize learning and to experience the reality of the Sport and Leisure environment. It should, therefore, be driven by the learning outcomes identified in our schemes of work and provide opportunities for our learners to achieve them. Again, they should be carefully prepared, in much the same way as we recommended for the visiting speakers so that their purpose is clear.

Then, of course, there is the organization of the visit for which most organizations will have a clear set of guidelines and protocols. Sometimes this can take longer than we might wish since the agreement of a number of stakeholders, such as Line Managers, Principals Governors and parents, has first to be established, so the importance of forward planning through the scheme of work is, again, essential. Figure 6.7 sets out a schedule of planning that you might find a useful guide to helping to make the visit an enjoyable, safe and meaningful learning experience.

Planning the Educational Visit

1. **Appraise the Benefits:**
    Is your trip really necessary? Senior managers, parents and learners need to know what the intended learning outcomes are.

2. **Check the Institutional Protocols:**
    What permissions are necessary? What forms are there to complete? How much notice is required? What are the conditions of the insurance cover?

3. **Identify any Potential Risks:**
    See previous discussion on risks but this can also include the prevailing weather conditions. It may be very hot or very cold at the destination: will the group be sufficiently prepared for this?

4. **Identify Participants' Needs:**
    Are there any health, dietary or fitness issues? Field trips can involve a lot of walking – are all members of the group up to it? Will there be any mobility issues (e.g. wheelchair access)? Take home contact numbers.

5. **Ratio of Staff to Students:**
    Check the protocols: 1:15 for trips at home 1:10 abroad. Take account of the gender mix, any special needs and the level of risk involved.

6. **Transport and Accommodation:**
    Plan the itinerary in detail and inform participants. Take special care if public transport is used: the London Underground can be daunting! If possible, check accommodation beforehand for health and safety and also proximity to other guests: a group of excited young adults can be irritating!

7. **Excursions:**
    Again, these should be well planned with clear objectives and the cost included in the overall package.

While on the trip

1. **Behaviour:**
    Expectations should be laid down beforehand and participants should sign an agreement and possible sanctions made clear. Be aware that alcohol can be a problem, and have clear policies about this.

2. **Keeping track of the group:**
    All members of the group must have an itinerary and contact numbers should they get lost (for once, mobile phones are invaluable!). Be aware and check numbers frequently.

3. **Unplanned events including possible injuries:**
    Make sure that you have contingency plans including emergency cash or credit someone who is First Aid trained and a Senior Management home contact.

Figure 6.7 Protocols for planning an educational visit

Reflection 6.11

Using the schedule of planning for an educational visit (Figure 6.7), draft out a plan for one (or both) of the visits suggested below, maximizing the benefits and minimizing the risks:

1   Plan to take a group of learners with which you are familiar to a major sports venue of your own choice for a day visit. The group might be 14-year-olds studying for GCSE or a Diploma, 17–19-year-olds on a ND programme or mature adults on a

> management programme, or any other group of your choosing. The visit might be
> to Wembley Stadium, or Twickenham, or the Manchester Cycle Velodrome: again
> the choice is yours.
> 2   Plan to take a group (again, of any age) on a residential visit to an adventurous
> outdoor activity centre. They are largely inexperienced in such activities, so the
> purpose is to broaden their experience of the Sport and Leisure industry.

Work-based learning as a teaching resource

The 2005, 14–19 Education and Skills White Paper (DfES) made work-related learning a compulsory element of the National Curriculum, whereby all students at Key Stage 4 are required to take part in a two-week period of work experience, and this is further built into the new Diplomas as a part of the learner's commitment to applied learning.

The Department for Educations and Skills, in 2002, defined work experience or Work Based Learning (WBL) as: 'a placement on an employer's premises in which a learner carries out a particular task or duty, more or less as would an employee, but with the emphasis on the learning aspects of the experience' (DfES 2002: 24).

The process of delivering industry-related work experience again requires preparation and careful implementation if it is to be meaningful. The sustainability of employer involvement is crucial to accommodate the increase in demand that is being experienced in England. Your school or college may have access to organizations that place all the learners in particular local education authority's area in placements or an in-house dedicated placement unit or department, but you will find in your area Education Business Partnerships (EBP), another useful source of work placements. The national network of EBP exists to make links between educational institutions and businesses and can be found in most regions. They will assist in finding employers willing to take learners on short-term placements: their website address is www.nebp.org.

Planning learning and assessment around WBL

To make the most of work-based learning, it is again essential that it is well planned and that the learners are fully prepared for the experience. For many it will be daunting and even disappointing since they will often be expected to carry out fairly menial tasks. But for younger learners there are a number of issues that limit what they can do. There may be legally imposed limits on the equipment that they can use and the kinds of tasks that they can perform. As we observed in Chapter 1, they may have ambitions to be sports coaches, personal trainers or physiotherapists, so having to wash down the changing room floors does not really fulfil their ambitions.

However, in the better placements, they will be given the opportunity to shadow other employees to see what they do and, if they show initiative, may even be given fairly responsible tasks. As one teacher suggested, one of the most valuable outcomes from work experience for young people is to see how adult employees behave in the workplace towards their work role, their peers and their managers.

Assessment for the work-based learning may be a requirement of the learner's programme as in the National Diploma for which there is a specific unit. Figure 6.8 is a summary of the unit content, but it does give a good guide.

The role of the teacher, then, is to plan the work-based learning experience to ensure that it meets the learning outcomes of the programme. The learning experience can focus on learning new skills; learning about the work environment, such as time keeping and working in teams; or learning about oneself. Once the key objectives have been decided, the method of capturing the learning by assessment has to be planned.

Figure 6.9 suggests how this might be planned to good effect. It is based on a model developed for students in Higher education, but we have adapted the principles for our purposes here.

Unit content

1 Know about the opportunities for work-based experience in sport
Opportunities: sectors, e.g. health and fitness, sport and recreation, outdoor education, sport and exercise sciences; providers, e.g. public sector, private sector, voluntary sector, partnerships
Types of occupation: opportunities in health and fitness, sport and recreation and the outdoors, e.g. sports scientist, exercise physiologist, bio-mechanist, sports psychologist, sports medicine, injury treatment, sports dietician, sports development officer, coaching and fitness, sports attendant, fitness instructor, PE teacher, sports coach, sports development officer, sports centre management, professional sports performer, sports promotion, sports ground facility worker, instructor; considerations, e.g. location, travel, cost, hours, regulations, health and safety, roles and responsibilities, development opportunities, progression, continued development

2 Be able to prepare for a work-based experience in sport
Prepare: aims and objectives; targets (specific, measurable, achievable, realistic, time-bound – SMART); personal, e.g. knowledge development, skills development, personal improvement, qualifications; organisational; relating to qualification/study, e.g. acquisition of knowledge, opportunity to gather supplementary evidence
Application process: job specifications; preparing required application documents, e.g. CV, application form, letter of application, personal statements, letters of acceptance/decline; interviews (preparation, skills)

3 Be able to undertake a work-based experience in sport
Undertake: planned activities; considerations, e.g. codes of practice, customer care, health and safety, legislation, regulation, equal opportunities, quality assurance, specific skills
Record: diary of daily activities; achievement of goals, aims and objectives (personal, organisational, relating to qualification/study)

4 Be able to evaluate a work-based experience in sport
Present: activities; achievements; formats, e.g. oral, written, use of ICT, graphics, written materials
Review: activities; achievements; achievement of goals, aims and objectives; strengths and areas for improvement; evidence and techniques, e.g. interviews and use of witness testimony; further goals, aims and objectives, e.g. experiences, training, qualifications

---

Figure 6.8 Exemplar unit for the assessment of work experience
Source: Unit 23: Work-based Experience in Sport

BN018434 – Specification – Edexcel Level 3 BTEC Nationals in Sport and Exercise Sciences – Issue 1 – October 2006 © Edexcel Limited 2006

Preparation for work-based learning	• Understanding the workplace environment • Preparing a CV/application form • Practice interviews • Meeting the employers – interviews? • Research the placement workplace • Expected behaviour
Developing WB learning plans	• What are the learning outcomes? • How can they be achieved? • Understanding your role • Drawing up a learning plan • What do you hope to learn? • How will you record your learning experience?
Learners on WBL	• Experience regular tasks in the environment • Observe other workers' behaviour • Research other aspects of the environment • Keep a record of observations and tasks • Complete assignment tasks
Learners return from WBL	• Write up assignment tasks • Review WBL log record of activities • Share experiences with the group • Presentations on WBL? • De-brief • Self-assessment
Assessment and feedback	• Employer reports • Assessment of assignment and logbook • Feedback from peers and teacher • Next steps

Figure 6.9 Making the most of work-based learning
Source: Based on Jenny Graham's model (2004).

Apart from the planning and the monitoring of the experience, as with most learning, perhaps the most valuable aspect is the reflection and debriefing afterwards to answer the question, 'What did you learn?' As we have suggested, this might best be achieved first through a presentation by the learner, and then by a plenary discussion between the whole group. Individual learners then can make up their minds as to how the experience has affected their perceptions of the industry and how it may have shaped their views on their own future.

Summary

In this final chapter we have tried to interpret 'resources' in the widest possible sense, but have been driven by our philosophy towards education in general reflected in our earlier discussions of the curriculum. If we believe that the learners are at the centre of the process and we believe that learning is an interactive process, then our views on the resources we choose to use, as Morrison and Ridley (1989) pointed out, will tend to be 'first hand' and available to our learners. We will seek to fully engage them with resources that contextualize their learning in the world of Sport and Leisure and also of the world with which they are familiar, which may, of course, vary according to their own life experiences. For many, though, this will mean a world of modern electronic media.

However, these resources are not merely ways of entertaining our learners, they must be carefully chosen to support and enhance their learning and to give it meaning. So they will give them the opportunity to experience first-hand aspects of Sport and Leisure whether experientially through work experience or taking part in activities in appropriate environments. To give credibility to our teaching of theory, we can refer to a range of expert sources, from advanced texts to the vast number of video clips readily available.

Our role in all this is to ensure that we keep abreast of developments and manage these resources to make learning both a challenging and enjoyable experience for our learners.

Glossary of acronyms

ALAN	Adult Literacy and Numeracy
BASE	British Association of Sport and Exercise Science
BIS	Department for Business, Innovation and Skills
BTEC	Business and Technical Education Council
CPD	Continued Professional Development
CSLA	Community Sports Leaders' Award
DCFS	Department for Children, Families and Schools
DfES	Department for Education and Schools
EBP	Education and Business Partnerships
ECM	Every Child Matters
GNVQ	General National Vocational Qualifications
HNC	Higher National Certificate
HND	Higher National Diploma
IfL	Institute for Learning
ISPAL	Institute for Sport, Parks and Leisure
ISRM	Institute of Sport and Recreation Management
(N)EBP	(National) Education and Business Partnerships
NIACE	National Institute of Adult and Continuing Education
NOCN	National Open College Network
NQF	National Qualifications Framework
NVQ	National Vocational Qualifications
PLTS	Personal Learning and Thinking Skills
QCA	Qualifications and Curriculum Authority
QCDA	Qualifications and Curriculum Development Agency
QCF	Qualifications and Credit Framework
ROSPA	Royal Society for the Prevention of Accidents

SIRC   Sport Industry Research Centre
SNVQ   Scottish National Vocational Qualifications
TDA   Teachers Development Agency
VLE   Virtual Learning Environment

Bibliography

Allison, L. (1998) Sport and Civil Society, in L. Allison (ed.) *Taking Sport Seriously*. Aachen: Meyer und Meyer.

Appleyard, N. and Appleyard, K. (2009) *The Minimum Core for Language and Literacy*. Exeter: Learning Matters Ltd.

Armitage, A., Bryant, R., Dunnill, R., Flannagan, K., Renwick, M., Hayes, D., Hudson, A., Kent, J. and Lawes, S. (2007) *Teaching and Training in Post-Compulsory Education*, 3rd edn. Maidenhead: Open University Press.

Armitage, A. and Renwick, M. (2007) *Assessment in FE*. London: Continuum.

Bandura, A. (1969) *Social Learning and Personality Development*. London: Holt, Rinehart and Winston.

Biggs, J. (2003) *Aligning Teaching and Assessment to Curriculum Objectives* (Imaginative Curriculum Project, LTSN Generic Centre).

Biggs, J. and Tang, C. (2007) *Teaching for Quality Learning*. Maidenhead: Open University Press.

Black, P. and Wiliam, D. (1998) *Inside the Black Box*. London: King's College.

Brookfield, S. (1998) *Becoming Critically Reflective Teachers*. San Francisco: Jossey-Bass.

Capel, S., Leask, M. and Turner, T. (2009) *Learning to Teach in the Secondary School*, 5th edn. Abingdon: Routledge.

Clarke, A. (2006) *Teaching Adults ICT Skills*. Exeter: Learning Matters.

Coffield, F., Ecclestone, K., Hall, E. and Moseley, D. (2004) *Learning Styles and Pedagogy in Post-16 Learning: A Systematic and Critical Review*. London: LSRC.

Dearing, R. (1996) *Review of Qualifications for 16–19 Year Olds* (Dearing II). Hayes: SCAA.

DfEE (1999) *A Fresh Start: Improving Literacy and Numeracy* (the Moser Report). London: HMSO.

DfEE (2006) *Prosperity for All in the Global Economy: World Class Skills* (The Leitch Report). Norwich: HMSO.

DfES (2002) *Work-Related Learning and the Law: Guidance for Schools and School-business Link Practitioners*. London: HMSO.

DfES (2007) *Raising Expectations: Staying in Education and Training Post-16*. London: HMSO.

DfES Standards Unit (2004) *Improving Differentiation in Business Education*. London: DfES.

DfES and QCA (1999) *Aims for the School Curriculum*. London: HMSO.

Donovan, G. (2005) *Teaching 14–19*. London: David Fulton.

Edexcel (2007) *Specifications for Level 3 BTEC Nationals in Sport and Exercise Sciences*. London: Edexcel.
Fegas, A. and Nicoll, K. (2008) *Foucault and Lifelong Learning*. Abingdon: Routledge.
Flemming, N.D. (2001) *Teaching and Learning Styles: VARK Strategies*. NZ: N.D. Flemming.
Freire, P. (1970) *Pedagogy of the Oppressed*. London: Continuum.
Gibbs, G. (1992) *Improving the Quality of Student Learning*. Plymouth: Technical and Educational Services Ltd.
Goodale, T. and Witt, P. (1991) *Recreation and Leisure: Issues in an Era of Change*. State College, PA: Venture Publishing.
Graham, J. (2004) *Reflective Portfolios for Work-Based Learning*. Available at: www.heacademy.ac.uk/assets/hlst/documents/LINK.Newsletter/Link11 (accessed 7 Feb. 2010).
Hargreaves, D., Hestar, S. and Mellor, F. (1975) *Deviance in Classrooms*. London: Routledge and Kegan Paul.
Hargreaves, J. (1987) *Sport, Power and Culture*. Cambridge: Polity Press.
Harkin, J.T., Turner, G. and Dawn, T. (2001) *Teaching Young Adults*. London: Routledge Falmer.
Honey, P. and Mumford, A. (1992) *The Manual of Learning Styles*. Maidenhead: P. Honey. Available at: http://www.parentscentre.gov.uk/schoollife/schooladministration/workexperience/.
Hyland, T. (1994) *Competence, Education and NVQs: Dissenting Perspectives*. London: Cassell.
Hyland, T. and Merrill, B. (2003) *The Changing Face of Further Education*. Abingdon: Routledge.
Jaques, D. and Salmon, G. (2007) *Learning in Groups*, 4th edn. London: Routledge.
Jarvie, G. (2006) *Sport, Culture and Society: An Introduction*. London: Routledge.
Knowles, M. (1984) *The Adult Learner: A Neglected Species*, 3rd edn. Houston, TX: Gulf Publishing.
Kolb, D.A. (1984) *Experiential Learning: Experience as the Source of Learning and Development*. London: Prentice Hall.
Lea, J., Armitage, A., Hayes, D., Lomas, L. and Markless, S. (2003) *Working in Post-Compulsory Education*. Maidenhead: Open University Press.
Lumby, J. and Foskett, N. (2005) *14–19 Education: Policy, Leadership and Learning*. London: Sage.
McDonald, J.P. (1992) Dilemmas of planning backwards: Rescuing a Good Idea, *Teachers' College Record* 94: 152–69.
Morrison, K. and Ridley, K. (1989) Curriculum ideologies, in M. Preedy, *Approaches to Curriculum Management*. Milton Keynes: Open University Press.
Mundy, J. (1998) *Leisure Education: Theory and Practice*, 2nd edn. Champaign, IL: Sagamore Publishing.
Nasta, T. (1994) *How to Design a Vocational Curriculum*. London: Kogan Page.
OCR (2008) *GCE Physical Education v2*. Nottingham: OCR Publications.
Peart, S. (2009) *The Minimum Core for Numeracy*. Exeter: Learning Matters.
Petty, G. (2009) *Teaching Today*, 4th edn. Cheltenham: Nelson Thornes.
QCA (2005) *A Review of GCE and GCSE Coursework Arrangements*. London: HMSO.
QCA (2007) *Functional Skills Standards*. London: QCA.
QCDA (2009) *Literacy, Numeracy and the Key Skills*. http://www.qcda.gov.uk/4537.aspx: (accessed 21 Oct. 2009).
Race, P. and Pickford, R. (2007) *Making Teaching Work*. London: Sage.
Reece, I. and Walker, S. (2007) *Teaching, Training and Learning: A Practical Guide*. Sunderland: Business Education Publications.

Royal Society for the Prevention of Accidents (1998) *Safety Education* (revised 2001). London: ROSPA.

Savage, J. (2008) *Teenage: The Creation of Youth Culture*. London: Pimlico.

Sport Industry Research Centre (SIRC) (2007) *The Economic Importance of Sport in England*. Sheffield: SIRC.

SPRITO (1997) *Coaching, Teaching and Instructing: National Occupational Standards Level 2. S/NVQ Guide*. London: SPRITO.

Stenhouse, L. (1975) *An Introduction to Curriculum Research and Development*. London: Heinemann.

Thomas, S., Smees, R., Macbeath, J. and Robertson, P. (2000) Valuing pupils' views in Scottish schools, *Educational Research and Evaluation*, 6(4): 281–316.

The Treasury Office (2003) *Every Child Matters*. London: HMSO.

Tummons, J. (2007) *Assessing Learning in the Lifelong Learning Sector*. Exeter: Learning Matters.

Tyler, R. (1971) *Basic Principles for Curriculum and Instruction*. Chicago: University of Chicago Press.

Vygotsky, L.S. (1978) *Thought and Language*. Cambridge, MA: Harvard University Press.

Wallace, S. (2005) *Teaching and Supporting Learning in Further Education: Meeting the FENTO Standards*. Exeter: Learning Matters.

Weston, P. (1992) 'A decade for differentiation', *BJSE*, xix (1).

Wiggins, G.P. (1993) *Assessing Student Performance*. San Francisco: Jossey-Bass.

Wolf, A. (2000) *Competency Based Assessment*. Buckingham: Open University Press.

Working Group on 14–19 Reform (2004) *14–19 Curriculum and Qualifications Reform* (the Tomlinson Report). Norwich: HMSO.

Websites

www.nocn.org.uk/about-us/mission%2c-vision-and-values (accessed 30 January 2010).

www.qca.org.uk/15525.html 'A review of GCE and GCSE coursework arrangements': (accessed 8 Feb. 2010).

www.qcda.gov.uk/4534.aspx (accessed 8 Feb. 2010).

www.rospa.com/safetyeducation/schooltrips/part2.htm, (accessed 7 Feb. 2010).

Index

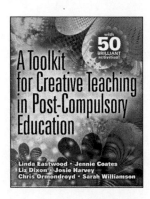

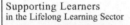

SUPPORTING LEARNERS IN THE LIFELONG LEARNING SECTOR

Marilyn Fairclough

978-0-335-23362-5 (Paperback)
2009

eBook also available

This is the first book of its kind to deal with the topic of supporting learners in PCET, rather than just focusing on how to teach them.

Key features:

- Each chapter cross-referenced to the QTLS Professional Standard for those on PTLLS, CTLLS and DTLLS courses
- Real life examples from a variety of settings and subjects
- Practical suggestions for developing classroom practice
- Suggestions for managing disruptive behaviour

www.openup.co.uk

OPEN UNIVERSITY PRESS
McGraw - Hill Education

**MODELS OF LEARNING,
TOOLS FOR TEACHING**
Third Edition

Bruce Joyce, Emily Calhoun
and David Hopkins

978-0-335-23419-6 (Paperback)
2008

eBook also available

This bestselling text provides a comprehensive and accessible
introduction to an array of models of teaching and learning.

Key features:

- A new chapter on teaching adolescents with disabilities to read
- A wealth of new scenarios and examples with clear guidelines for
  implementation
- New research and illustrations
- A revised Picture Word Inductive Model

www.openup.co.uk

OPEN UNIVERSITY PRESS
McGraw · Hill Education